DEUTERONOMY

THE IGNATIUS CATHOLIC STUDY BIBLE

REVISED STANDARD VERSION
SECOND CATHOLIC EDITION

DEUTERONOMY

Introduction, Commentary, and Notes
by Scott Hahn and Curtis Mitch

with

Michael Barber

and with

Study Questions by Dennis Walters

IGNATIUS PRESS   SAN FRANCISCO

Original Bible text: Revised Standard Version, Catholic Edition
Nihil Obstat: Thomas Hanlon, S.T.L., L.S.S., Ph.L.
Imprimatur: + Peter W. Bartholome, D.D.
Bishop of Saint Cloud, Minnesota
May 11, 1966

Introduction, commentaries, and notes:
Nihil Obstat: Ruth Ohm Sutherland, Ph.D., Censor Deputatus
Imprimatur: + The Most Reverend Salvatore Cordileone
Archbishop of San Francisco
January 10, 2020

Cover art: Painting by Jacques Joseph Tissot
The Jewish Museum, New York
Art Resource, N.Y.

Cover design by Riz Boncan Marsella

Published by Ignatius Press in 2021

CONTENTS

Introduction to the Ignatius Study Bible, by Scott Hahn, Ph.D. 7

Introduction to Deuteronomy 13

 Outline of Deuteronomy 16

Annotations on Deuteronomy 17

 Word Study: *Loved* 23

 Topical Essay: What Is a Covenant? 24

 Word Study: *Possession* 28

 Word Study: *Heart* 54

Study Questions: Deuteronomy 63

Books of the Bible 75

INTRODUCTION TO
THE IGNATIUS STUDY BIBLE
by Scott Hahn, Ph.D.

You are approaching the "word of God". This is the title Christians most commonly give to the Bible, and the expression is rich in meaning. It is also the title given to the Second Person of the Blessed Trinity, God the Son. For Jesus Christ became flesh for our salvation, and "the name by which he is called is The Word of God" (Rev 19:13; cf. Jn 1:14).

The word of God is Scripture. The Word of God is Jesus. This close association between God's *written* word and his *eternal* Word is intentional and has been the custom of the Church since the first generation. "All Sacred Scripture is but one book, and this one book is Christ, 'because all divine Scripture speaks of Christ, and all divine Scripture is fulfilled in Christ' [1] " (CCC 134). This does not mean that the Scriptures are divine in the same way that Jesus is divine. They are, rather, divinely inspired and, as such, are unique in world literature, just as the Incarnation of the eternal Word is unique in human history.

Yet we can say that the inspired word resembles the incarnate Word in several important ways. Jesus Christ is the Word of God incarnate. In his humanity, he is like us in all things, except for sin. As a work of man, the Bible is like any other book, except without error. Both Christ and Scripture, says the Second Vatican Council, are given "for the sake of our salvation" (*Dei Verbum* 11), and both give us God's definitive revelation of himself. We cannot, therefore, conceive of one without the other: the Bible without Jesus, or Jesus without the Bible. Each is the interpretive key to the other. And because Christ is the subject of all the Scriptures, St. Jerome insists, "Ignorance of the Scriptures is ignorance of Christ" [2] (CCC 133).

When we approach the Bible, then, we approach Jesus, the Word of God; and in order to encounter Jesus, we must approach him in a prayerful study of the inspired word of God, the Sacred Scriptures.

Inspiration and Inerrancy The Catholic Church makes mighty claims for the Bible, and our acceptance of those claims is essential if we are to read the Scriptures and apply them to our lives as the Church intends. So it is not enough merely to nod at words like "inspired", "unique", or "inerrant". We have to understand what the Church means by these terms, and we have to make that understanding our own. After all, what we believe about the Bible will inevitably influence the way we read the Bible. The way we read the Bible, in turn, will determine what we "get out" of its sacred pages.

These principles hold true no matter what we read: a news report, a search warrant, an advertisement, a paycheck, a doctor's prescription, an eviction notice. How (or whether) we read these things depends largely upon our preconceived notions about the reliability and authority of their sources—and the potential they have for affecting our lives. In some cases, to misunderstand a document's authority can lead to dire consequences. In others, it can keep us from enjoying rewards that are rightfully ours. In the case of the Bible, both the rewards and the consequences involved take on an ultimate value.

What does the Church mean, then, when she affirms the words of St. Paul: "All Scripture is inspired by God" (2 Tim 3:16)? Since the term "inspired" in this passage could be translated "God-breathed", it follows that God breathed forth his word in the Scriptures as you and I breathe forth air when we speak. This means that God is the primary author of the Bible. He certainly employed human authors in this task as well, but he did not merely assist them while they wrote or subsequently approve what they had written. God the Holy Spirit is the *principal* author of Scripture, while the human writers are *instrumental* authors. These human authors freely wrote everything, and only those things, that God wanted: the word of God in the very words of God. This miracle of dual authorship extends to the whole of Scripture, and to every one of its parts, so that whatever the human authors affirm, God likewise affirms through their words.

The principle of biblical inerrancy follows logically from this principle of divine authorship. After all, God cannot lie, and he cannot make mistakes. Since the Bible is divinely inspired, it must be without error in everything that its divine and human authors affirm to be true. This means that biblical inerrancy is a mystery even broader in scope than infallibility, which guarantees for us that the Church will always teach the truth concerning faith and morals. Of course the mantle of inerrancy likewise covers faith and morals, but it extends even farther to ensure that all the facts and events of salvation history are accurately presented for us in

---

[1] Hugh of St. Victor, *De arca Noe* 2, 8: PL 176, 642: cf. ibid. 2, 9: PL 176, 642–43.

[2] *DV* 25; cf. Phil 3:8 and St. Jerome, *Commentariorum in Isaiam libri xviii*, prol.: PL 24, 17b.

the Scriptures. Inerrancy is our guarantee that the words and deeds of God found in the Bible are unified and true, declaring with one voice the wonders of his saving love.

The guarantee of inerrancy does not mean, however, that the Bible is an all-purpose encyclopedia of information covering every field of study. The Bible is not, for example, a textbook in the empirical sciences, and it should not be treated as one. When biblical authors relate facts of the natural order, we can be sure they are speaking in a purely descriptive and "phenomenological" way, according to the way things appeared to their senses.

Biblical Authority Implicit in these doctrines is God's desire to make himself known to the world and to enter a loving relationship with every man, woman, and child he has created. God gave us the Scriptures not just to inform or motivate us; more than anything he wants to save us. This higher purpose underlies every page of the Bible, indeed every word of it.

In order to reveal himself, God used what theologians call "accommodation". Sometimes the Lord stoops down to communicate by "condescension"— that is, he speaks as humans speak, as if he had the same passions and weakness that we do (for example, God says he was "sorry" that he made man in Genesis 6:6). Other times he communicates by "elevation"—that is, by endowing human words with divine power (for example, through the Prophets). The numerous examples of divine accommodation in the Bible are an expression of God's wise and fatherly ways. For a sensitive father can speak with his children either by condescension, as in baby talk, or by elevation, by bringing a child's understanding up to a more mature level.

God's word is thus saving, fatherly, and personal. Because it speaks directly to us, we must never be indifferent to its content; after all, the word of God is at once the object, cause, and support of our faith. It is, in fact, a test of our faith, since we see in the Scriptures only what faith disposes us to see. If we believe what the Church believes, we will see in Scripture the saving, inerrant, and divinely authored revelation of the Father. If we believe otherwise, we see another book altogether.

This test applies not only to rank-and-file believers but also to the Church's theologians and hierarchy, and even the Magisterium. Vatican II has stressed in recent times that Scripture must be "the very soul of sacred theology" (*Dei Verbum* 24). As Joseph Cardinal Ratzinger, Pope Benedict XVI echoed this powerful teaching with his own, insisting that "the *normative theologians* are the authors of Holy Scripture" (emphasis added). He reminded us that Scripture and the Church's dogmatic teaching are tied tightly together, to the point of being inseparable: "Dogma is by definition nothing other than an interpretation of Scripture." The defined dogmas of our faith, then, encapsulate the Church's infallible interpretation of Scripture, and theology is a further reflection upon that work.

The Senses of Scripture Because the Bible has both divine and human authors, we are required to master a different sort of reading than we are used to. First, we must read Scripture according to its *literal* sense, as we read any other human literature. At this initial stage, we strive to discover the meaning of the words and expressions used by the biblical writers as they were understood in their original setting and by their original recipients. This means, among other things, that we do not interpret everything we read "literalistically", as though Scripture never speaks in a figurative or symbolic way (it often does!). Rather, we read it according to the rules that govern its different literary forms of writing, depending on whether we are reading a narrative, a poem, a letter, a parable, or an apocalyptic vision. The Church calls us to read the divine books in this way to ensure that we understand what the human authors were laboring to explain to God's people.

The literal sense, however, is not the only sense of Scripture, since we interpret its sacred pages according to the *spiritual* senses as well. In this way, we search out what the Holy Spirit is trying to tell us, beyond even what the human authors have consciously asserted. Whereas the literal sense of Scripture describes a historical reality—a fact, precept, or event—the spiritual senses disclose deeper mysteries revealed through the historical realities. What the soul is to the body, the spiritual senses are to the literal. You can distinguish them; but if you try to separate them, death immediately follows. St. Paul was the first to insist upon this and warn of its consequences: "God ... has qualified us to be ministers of a new covenant, not in a written code but in the Spirit; for the written code kills, but the Spirit gives life" (2 Cor 3:5–6).

Catholic tradition recognizes three spiritual senses that stand upon the foundation of the literal sense of Scripture (see CCC 115). **(1)** The first is the *allegorical* sense, which unveils the spiritual and prophetic meaning of biblical history. Allegorical interpretations thus reveal how persons, events, and institutions of Scripture can point beyond themselves toward greater mysteries yet to come (OT) or display the fruits of mysteries already revealed (NT). Christians have often read the Old Testament in this way to discover how the mystery of Christ in the New Covenant was once hidden in the Old and how the full significance of the Old Covenant was finally made manifest in the New. Allegorical significance is likewise latent in the New Testament, especially in the life and deeds of Jesus recorded in the Gospels. Because Christ is the Head of the Church and the source of her spiritual life, what was accomplished in Christ the Head during his earthly life prefigures what he continually produces in his members through grace. The allegorical sense builds up the virtue of faith. **(2)** The second is the *tropological* or *moral* sense, which reveals how the actions of God's people in the Old Testament and the life of Jesus in the New Testament prompt us to form virtuous habits in our own lives. It therefore draws from Scripture warnings against sin and vice as well as inspirations to pursue holiness and purity. The moral sense is intended to build up the virtue of charity. **(3)** The third is the *anagogical* sense, which points upward to heavenly glory. It shows us how countless events in the Bible prefigure our final union with God in eternity and how things that are "seen" on earth are figures of things "unseen" in heaven. Because the anagogical sense leads us to contemplate our destiny, it is meant to build up the virtue of hope. Together with the literal sense, then, these spiritual senses draw out the fullness of what God wants to give us through his word and as such comprise what ancient tradition has called the "full sense" of Sacred Scripture.

All of this means that the deeds and events of the Bible are charged with meaning beyond what is immediately apparent to the reader. In essence, that meaning is Jesus Christ and the salvation he died to give us. This is especially true of the books of the New Testament, which proclaim Jesus explicitly; but it is also true of the Old Testament, which speaks of Jesus in more hidden and symbolic ways. The human authors of the Old Testament told us as much as they were able, but they could not clearly discern the shape of all future events standing at such a distance. It is the Bible's divine Author, the Holy Spirit, who could and did foretell the saving work of Christ, from the first page of the Book of Genesis onward.

The New Testament did not, therefore, abolish the Old. Rather, the New fulfilled the Old, and in doing so, it lifted the veil that kept hidden the face of the Lord's bride. Once the veil is removed, we suddenly see the world of the Old Covenant charged with grandeur. Water, fire, clouds, gardens, trees, hills, doves, lambs—all of these things are memorable details in the history and poetry of Israel. But now, seen in the light of Jesus Christ, they are much more. For the Christian with eyes to see, water symbolizes the saving power of Baptism; fire, the Holy Spirit; the spotless lamb, Christ crucified; Jerusalem, the city of heavenly glory.

The spiritual reading of Scripture is nothing new. Indeed, the very first Christians read the Bible this way. St. Paul describes Adam as a "type" that prefigured Jesus Christ (Rom 5:14). A "type" is a real person, place, thing, or event in the Old Testament that foreshadows something greater in the New. From this term we get the word "typology", referring to the study of how the Old Testament prefigures Christ (CCC 128–30). Elsewhere St. Paul draws deeper meanings out of the story of Abraham's sons, declaring, "This is an allegory" (Gal 4:24). He is not suggesting that these events of the distant past never really happened; he is saying that the events both happened *and* signified something more glorious yet to come.

The New Testament later describes the Tabernacle of ancient Israel as "a copy and shadow of the heavenly sanctuary" (Heb 8:5) and the Mosaic Law as a "shadow of the good things to come" (Heb 10:1). St. Peter, in turn, notes that Noah and his family were "saved through water" in a way that "corresponds" to sacramental Baptism, which "now saves you" (1 Pet 3:20–21). It is interesting to note that the expression translated as "corresponds" in this verse is a Greek term that denotes the fulfillment or counterpart of an ancient "type".

We need not look to the apostles, however, to justify a spiritual reading of the Bible. After all, Jesus himself read the Old Testament this way. He referred to Jonah (Mt 12:39), Solomon (Mt 12:42), the Temple (Jn 2:19), and the brazen serpent (Jn 3:14) as "signs" that pointed forward to him. We see in Luke's Gospel, as Christ comforted the disciples on the road to Emmaus, that "beginning with Moses and all the prophets, he interpreted to them in all the Scriptures the things concerning himself" (Lk 24:27). It was precisely this extensive spiritual interpretation of the Old Testament that made such an impact on these once-discouraged travelers, causing their hearts to "burn" within them (Lk 24:32).

Criteria for Biblical Interpretation We, too, must learn to discern the "full sense" of Scripture as it includes both the literal and spiritual senses together. Still, this does not mean we should "read into" the Bible meanings that are not really there. Spiritual exegesis is not an unrestrained flight of the imagination. Rather, it is a sacred science that proceeds according to certain principles and stands accountable to sacred tradition, the Magisterium, and the wider community of biblical interpreters (both living and deceased).

In searching out the full sense of a text, we should always avoid the extreme tendency to "over-spiritualize" in a way that minimizes or denies the Bible's literal truth. St. Thomas Aquinas was well aware of this danger and asserted that "all other senses of Sacred Scripture are based on the literal" (*STh* I, 1, 10, *ad* 1, quoted in CCC 116). On the other hand, we should never confine the meaning of a text to the literal, intended sense of its human author, as if the divine Author did not intend the passage to be read in the light of Christ's coming.

Fortunately the Church has given us guidelines in our study of Scripture. The unique character and divine authorship of the Bible call us to read it "in the Spirit" (*Dei Verbum* 12). Vatican II outlines this teaching in a practical way by directing us to read the Scriptures according to three specific criteria:

1. We must "[b]e especially attentive 'to the content and unity of the whole Scripture'" (CCC 112).

2. We must "[r]ead the Scripture within 'the living Tradition of the whole Church'" (CCC 113).

3. We must "[b]e attentive to the analogy of faith" (CCC 114; cf. Rom 12:6).

These criteria protect us from many of the dangers that ensnare readers of the Bible, from the newest inquirer to the most prestigious scholar. Reading Scripture out of context is one such pitfall, and probably the one most difficult to avoid. A memorable cartoon from the 1950s shows a young man poring over the pages of the Bible. He says to his sister: "Don't bother me now; I'm trying to find a Scripture verse to back up one of my preconceived notions." No doubt a biblical text pried from its context can be twisted to say something very different from what its author actually intended.

The Church's criteria guide us here by defining what constitutes the authentic "context" of a given biblical passage. The first criterion directs us to the literary context of every verse, including not only the words and paragraphs that surround it, but also the entire corpus of the biblical author's writings and, indeed, the span of the entire Bible. The *complete* literary context of any Scripture verse includes every text from Genesis to Revelation—because the Bible is a unified book, not just a library of different books. When the Church canonized the Book of Revelation, for example, she recognized it to be incomprehensible apart from the wider context of the entire Bible.

The second criterion places the Bible firmly within the context of a community that treasures a "living tradition". That community is the People of God down through the ages. Christians lived out their faith for well over a millennium before the printing press was invented. For centuries, few believers owned copies of the Gospels, and few people could read anyway. Yet they absorbed the gospel—through the sermons of their bishops and clergy, through prayer and meditation, through Christian art, through liturgical celebrations, and through oral tradition. These were expressions of the one "living tradition", a culture of living faith that stretches from ancient Israel to the contemporary Church. For the early Christians, the gospel could not be understood apart from that tradition. So it is with us. Reverence for the Church's tradition is what protects us from any sort of chronological or cultural provincialism, such as scholarly fads that arise and carry away a generation of interpreters before being dismissed by the next generation.

The third criterion places scriptural texts within the framework of faith. If we believe that the Scriptures are divinely inspired, we must also believe them to be internally coherent and consistent with all the doctrines that Christians believe. Remember, the Church's dogmas (such as the Real Presence,

the papacy, the Immaculate Conception) are not something *added* to Scripture; rather, they are the Church's infallible interpretation *of* Scripture.

Using This Study Guide This volume is designed to lead the reader through Scripture according to the Church's guidelines—faithful to the canon, to the tradition, and to the creeds. The Church's interpretive principles have thus shaped the component parts of this book, and they are designed to make the reader's study as effective and rewarding as possible.

Introductions: We have introduced the biblical book with an essay covering issues such as authorship, date of composition, purpose, and leading themes. This background information will assist readers to approach and understand the text on its own terms.

Annotations: The basic notes at the bottom of every page help the user to read the Scriptures with understanding. They by no means exhaust the meaning of the sacred text but provide background material to help the reader make sense of what he reads. Often these notes make explicit what the sacred writers assumed or held to be implicit. They also provide a great deal of historical, cultural, geographical, and theological information pertinent to the inspired narratives—information that can help the reader bridge the distance between the biblical world and his own.

Cross-References: Between the biblical text at the top of each page and the annotations at the bottom, numerous references are listed to point readers to other scriptural passages related to the one being studied. This follow-up is an essential part of any serious study. It is also an excellent way to discover how the content of Scripture "hangs together" in a providential unity. Along with biblical cross-references, the annotations refer to select paragraphs from the *Catechism of the Catholic Church*. These are not doctrinal "proof texts" but are designed to help the reader interpret the Bible in accordance with the mind of the Church. The *Catechism* references listed either handle the biblical text directly or treat a broader doctrinal theme that sheds significant light on that text.

Topical Essays, Word Studies, Charts: These features bring readers to a deeper understanding of select details. The *topical essays* take up major themes and explain them more thoroughly and theologically than the annotations, often relating them to the doctrines of the Church. Occasionally the annotations are supplemented by *word studies* that put readers in touch with the ancient languages of Scripture. These should help readers to understand better and appreciate the inspired terminology that runs throughout the sacred books. Also included are various *charts* that summarize biblical information "at a glance".

Icon Annotations: Three distinctive icons are interspersed throughout the annotations, each one corresponding to one of the Church's three criteria for biblical interpretation. Bullets indicate the passage or passages to which these icons apply.

📖 Notes marked by the book icon relate to the "content and unity" of Scripture, showing how particular passages of the Old Testament illuminate the mysteries of the New. Much of the information in these notes explains the original context of the citations and indicates how and why this has a direct bearing on Christ or the Church. Through these notes, the reader can develop a sensitivity to the beauty and unity of God's saving plan as it stretches across both Testaments.

🕊 Notes marked by the dove icon examine particular passages in light of the Church's "living tradition". Because the Holy Spirit both guides the Magisterium and inspires the spiritual senses of Scripture, these annotations supply information along both of these lines. On the one hand, they refer to the Church's doctrinal teaching as presented by various popes, creeds, and ecumenical councils; on the other, they draw from (and paraphrase) the spiritual interpretations of various Fathers, Doctors, and saints.

🔑 Notes marked by the keys icon pertain to the "analogy of faith". Here we spell out how the mysteries of our faith "unlock" and explain one another. This type of comparison between Christian beliefs displays the coherence and unity of defined dogmas, which are the Church's infallible interpretations of Scripture.

Putting It All in Perspective Perhaps the most important context of all we have saved for last: the interior life of the individual reader. What we get out of the Bible will largely depend on how we approach the Bible. Unless we are living a sustained and disciplined life of prayer, we will never have the reverence, the profound humility, or the grace we need to see the Scriptures for what they really are.

You are approaching the "word of God". But for thousands of years, since before he knit you in your mother's womb, the Word of God has been approaching you.

One Final Note. The volume you hold in your hands is only a small part of a much larger work still in production. Study helps similar to those printed in this booklet are being prepared for *all* the books of the Bible and will appear gradually as they are finished. Our ultimate goal is to publish a single, one-volume Study Bible that will include the entire text of Scripture, along with all the annotations, charts, cross-references, maps, and other features found in the following pages. Individual booklets will be published in the meantime, with the hope that God's people can begin to benefit from this labor before its full completion.

We have included a long list of Study Questions in the back to make this format as useful as possible, not only for individual study, but for group settings and discussions as well. The questions are designed to help readers both "understand" the Bible and "apply" it to their lives. We pray that God will make use of our efforts and yours to help renew the face of the earth! «

INTRODUCTION TO DEUTERONOMY

Author and Date Deuteronomy presents itself as a collection of farewell sermons delivered by Moses (1:1, 3, 5, etc.) that he himself put into writing before his death (31:9, 22, 24). Based on this information, centuries of Jewish and Christian tradition have identified Moses as the author of the book. It follows, if one accepts the internal claim of Mosaic authorship, that at least the speeches of Deuteronomy must be dated near the end of Moses' lifetime in the late 1400s B.C. (or possibly the 1200s). The setting of Deuteronomy is consistent with the historical situation at this time, with the twelve tribes of Israel united as a people recently freed from Egypt and ready to enter the land of Canaan.

Modern scholarship has developed different views on the composition of Deuteronomy. Critical scholars typically attribute the book to the activity of spiritual leaders who lived during the late monarchical period, between roughly 800 and 600 B.C. The authors are thought to have been either *prophets* from northern Israel, Levitical *priests* from northern Israel who fled south to the Southern Kingdom of Judah, or royal *scribes* working in Jerusalem. Most hold that some form of Deuteronomy (especially the law code of Deut 12–26) played a significant role in the religious reforms of King Josiah in 622 B.C. (discovered as "the book of the law" in 2 Kings 22:8). It is the majority opinion among critical scholars today that Deuteronomy reached its final form around the time of the Babylonian Exile in the sixth century B.C.

Several observations underlie this modern position. **(1)** Deuteronomy concludes with a brief account of the death and burial of Moses (34:5–8) along with a retrospective remark that "there has not arisen a prophet since in Israel like Moses" (34:10). Both passages seem to imply that someone other than Moses, presumably someone who lived long after the time of Moses, authored the book. **(2)** Scholars have noted that several of Josiah's religious reforms in the late seventh century appear to be direct responses to the laws of Deuteronomy, e.g., the destruction of pagan shrines throughout the land (compare 12:2–3 with 2 Kings 23:4–20), the elimination of occult practices such as sorcery and child sacrifice (compare 18:10–11 with 2 Kings 23:10, 24), and Israel's national celebration of Passover at the central sanctuary (compare 16:1–8 with 2 Kings 23:21–22). Since the Bible's historical books do not suggest that such a wide-ranging implementation of Deuteronomy was attempted before Josiah's time, it is inferred that the book first appeared as an authoritative document during Josiah's reign from 640–609 B.C. **(3)** Comparative studies have identified parallels in wording between the curses of the covenant in Deut 28:15–68 and select curses in the Assyrian vassal treaties of Esarhaddon, who reigned from 681–669 B.C. These parallels are readily explained if Deuteronomy was composed in the seventh century B.C.

Despite the prevalence of this modern account, there are balancing considerations that suggest an origin for Deuteronomy in more ancient times. Among these considerations are the following: **(1)** Deuteronomy is silent about major events and institutions of the post-Mosaic period that a book composed in the seventh century B.C. might be expected to include, e.g., no mention is made of Jerusalem as the site chosen by God for Israel's central sanctuary; nothing is said about David and his royal successors as the kings chosen by God to rule on Zion; there is no sign that the author of the book had knowledge of the breakup of Israel's once-united tribes into Northern and Southern Kingdoms in 930 B.C. These issues loomed large in the period of the divided monarchy, and yet they go unmentioned in Deuteronomy. **(2)** The book cautions the Israelites against fostering close relationships with the indigenous peoples of Canaan who occupied the Promised Land before Israel's arrival (7:1–5). Evidence is lacking, however, that the peoples named in Deuteronomy remained as identifiable groups in the land of Israel into the seventh century. During this later period of biblical history, Israel faced, not internal foreign threats from Canaanites, but external threats from peoples such as the Babylonians, Ammonites, Moabites, and Phoenicians. **(3)** The command to ratify the Deuteronomic covenant by building an altar on Mt. Ebal in Samaria (27:1–8) runs directly counter to the reforms of Josiah in the seventh century, when a campaign was launched to demolish every cultic sanctuary and altar except the national Temple in Jerusalem (2 Kings 23:4–20). **(4)** Deuteronomy exhibits parallels in form and substance with international Hittite treaties that date back to the second half of the second millennium B.C. These are Near Eastern political arrangements in which a conquering king (suzerain) imposed a covenant of exclusive loyalty upon a subject nation (vassal). Because this treaty format changed over the centuries, and a slightly different model was current in the period of Assyrian dominance in the first millennium B.C., there is good reason to think that the covenantal structure of Deuteronomy originated in the second rather than the first millennium. Analysis confirms that parallels between Deuteronomy and the older Hittite treaties, while not always exact, are more numerous and substantial than parallels identified between the curses in Deuteronomy and the curses in the later Assyrian treaties of Esarhaddon. For the characteristic features of this treaty format, see *Structure*.

Perhaps the best solution to the question of Deuteronomy's origin is the most inclusive one. Virtually all the evidence cited in support of the traditional and modern positions can be accounted for if the Book of Deuteronomy reached its final form in stages. One might theorize, for instance, that a covenant document, designed as a charter for the newly founded nation of Israel, was produced by an educated leader such as Moses in the second half of the second millennium B.C. An authoritative document such as this might then undergo slight modification and expansion in later times. For instance, it seems reasonable to hold that an unknown editor added narrative and homiletical material to the book, including Moses' obituary and the praise of Moses' greatness in Deut 34; likewise, someone living in the period of Assyrian rule may have edited the curses in Deut 28 to evoke threats against rebel nations that were familiar to readers at this later time. There is no reason to doubt, then, that Deuteronomy was a major force behind King Josiah's reform in 622 B.C. But this does not require that the book was written during Josiah's reign; it requires only that the Deuteronomic laws existed and attracted renewed attention during his reign. It is thus reasonable to surmise, in view of the juxtaposition of early and late features in the book, that the substance of Deuteronomy originated at the time of Israel's founding as a nation, even if adjustments and additions were made to the book in subsequent centuries, perhaps as late as the reign of Josiah or even the Babylonian Exile.

Title The Hebrew heading for Deuteronomy consists of its opening words, *'elleh haddebarim*, "these are the words" (1:1). This title captures nicely the essence of the book, which claims to record the spoken discourse of Moses. The Greek Septuagint entitles the work *Deuteronomion*, which means "second law" and represents a free translation of "a copy of this law" in 17:18. This, too, is an apt title, since Deuteronomy constitutes a second covenant under Moses that was set forth on the plains of Moab forty years after the Lord ratified his first covenant with Israel at Mt. Sinai (29:1). English Bibles typically follow the Greek rather than the Hebrew tradition, as does the Latin Vulgate with the heading *Liber Deuteronomii*, "Book of Deuteronomy".

Structure Deuteronomy exhibits a five-part structure that corresponds to a Near Eastern vassal treaty. It most closely resembles the Hittite model that was current between ca. 1400 and 1200 B.C., although minor differences in order indicate that Deuteronomy does not adhere to this treaty format in a rigid way. **(1)** The book begins with a *preamble* that identifies the Lord as the king or suzerain who initiates the covenant with his vassal subjects, the children of Israel (1:1–5). **(2)** This is followed by a *historical prologue* that summarizes the suzerain's past relationship with the vassal, highlighting his beneficence (1:6—4:43). **(3)** The *stipulations* of the covenant, cast in the form of general and specific demands, are then laid upon the vassal (4:44—26:19). **(4)** The *sanctions* set forth the blessings and curses of the covenant, i.e., the consequences of obedience and disobedience to the treaty stipulations. **(5)** Several *succession arrangements* are made that invoke witnesses, provide for the storage of the covenant document, and set a schedule for the periodic rereading of its contents (31:1—34:12).

Content and Themes Deuteronomy stands at a turning point in the biblical story. The Exodus from slavery in Egypt has been accomplished, forty years of wandering in the wilderness have come to an end, and Israel stands on the plains of Moab within eyesight of the Promised Land. Now, at long last, the children of those who came up out of Egypt are poised to succeed where their parents had failed by crossing into the land of Canaan and claiming it as their inheritance. This is the generation addressed by Deuteronomy, a generation that is about to begin a new life in a new land.

To prepare them for this, Moses delivers passionate preaching about the responsibilities of living as the People of God. He warns the twelve tribes of the challenges they will face in the future and urges them to be mindful of the lessons of the past. Above all, Moses proclaims the Lord's love for Israel and makes powerful appeals for Israel to return his love by loyal obedience to the covenant. This message is expressed through historical narration and legislation as well as in homily and prophecy.

Deuteronomy is thus unique among the books of the Pentateuch for the prominence it gives to the voice of Moses. In contrast to the stories in Exodus, Leviticus, and Numbers, where Moses hears the voice of the Lord—on the summit of Mt. Sinai or within the sanctuary—and then conveys what he has heard to the Israelites (Ex 19:3–9; Lev 1:1–2; Num 7:89), Deuteronomy describes the voice of the Lord as a memory from days gone by (4:11–13; 5:4–5, 22–27). The only *audible* voice that sounds forth in Deuteronomy is that of Moses (1:1; 4:1–2; 29:1; 31:1, 7, 10–13, 30; etc.). The divine inspiration of the book is not thereby minimized or denied; rather, the role of Moses as a covenant mediator is magnified.

The primary function of the book is threefold:

(1) Deuteronomy is first of all a *covenant document*. This is clear from the way it adopts the structure of a Near Eastern vassal treaty, in which a mighty king asserts his sovereignty over a subject people, imposes an oath of loyalty upon them, and sets forth the blessings and curses that will follow when a vassal proves loyal or disloyal. In the conventional terminology of these treaties, the suzerain is a "father" to the vassal, and the vassal becomes his "son". Deuteronomy conforms to this model by casting the Lord as the divine "king" (33:5) who places Israel under oaths of allegiance (27:15–26) and holds out the prospect of blessings and curses for obedience and disobedience (28:1–68). Not only does the Lord demand exclusive loyalty from Israel, as a suzerain did of his vassal (4:15–40; 5:6–7; 26:17), but the relationship between them is that of a Father and his son (1:31; 8:5; 14:1; 32:6, 19–20). Imitation of these ancient treaties implies that Deuteronomy places Israel, after years of rebellion in the wilderness (9:7), in a state of covenant vassalage. For the duration of its national life, Israel will be governed by the strict discipline of the Deuteronomic covenant under the watchful eye of the Lord.

(2) Deuteronomy is also a *national constitution*. It is a charter for Israel's life in the land of Canaan. In contrast to Exodus, Leviticus, and Numbers, which are dominated by ceremonial and ethical laws related to personal life and public worship, Deuteronomy gives greater focus to the civic dimensions of Israel's life. It thus makes provision for national government in the form of a monarchy, judiciary, and clergy. A king will be established over the tribes of Israel, but his power will be strictly regulated by the laws of Deuteronomy, which he is expected to study and embody as a model citizen (17:14–20). Judges in Israel will serve on local courts (16:18–20) as well as on a national tribunal (17:8–13), following the guidelines given in Deuteronomy for judicial procedure and criminal correction (19:15–21; 25:1–3). The Levitical ministers of worship are the custodians of the Deuteronomic law code (17:18; 31:9); they are responsible for instructing the people, for facilitating the worship of the people, and, in return for their services, they are entitled to receive tithes and offerings from the people (18:1–8; 33:10). On economic matters, laws are given to regulate the cancellation of debts (15:1–3), the collection of interest on loans (23:19–20), fair business practices (25:13–16), and tithes owed to the Levites (14:22–29). Laws pertaining to domestic life deal with divorce and remarriage (24:1–4), the inheritance of family property (21:15–17), the punishment of rebellious children (21:18–21), and the prosecution of sexual crimes such as adultery, rape, and incest (22:22–30). Military policies are outlined for combat exemptions in wartime (20:1–9) as well as foreign and domestic conflicts (20:10–20). In these ways, Deuteronomy welds piety and patriotism together, so that faith and life form a unity in the everyday affairs of the covenant people. Obedience to the Lord is the sure path to prosperity and international prominence for Israel (7:12–16; 28:1–14), while disobedience—especially idolatry—is the greatest threat to Israel's national security in the land (4:25–28; 28:15–68).

(3) Deuteronomy is also a *distinct Mosaic law code*. It restates several laws already given to Israel, such as the Ten Commandments, but it also adds new or modified ones that are not attested in earlier legislation. In some cases, Deuteronomy introduces entirely new laws, such as the release of debts every seven years (15:1–3). In other cases, it adds new requirements to old laws, such as the one to grant parting provisions to a newly released slave (compare 15:12–18 with Ex 21:1–11). Several times it adapts old laws to the new situation of Israel living in the land of Canaan, as when Israel's religious festivals, previously instituted in Exodus, Leviticus, and Numbers, are made pilgrimage feasts that require Israelites dispersed throughout the land to worship at the central sanctuary (16:1–16). Perhaps most distinctive of all, Deuteronomy makes several legal concessions to the moral and spiritual weaknesses of Israel as demonstrated during the wilderness period. These are downward adjustments that lower the level of expectation for a people struggling to live by the high standards of the Sinai covenant. Laws in this category include the toleration of divorce and remarriage (24:1–4), the permission to collect interest on loans made to Gentiles (15:3; 23:19–20), the mandate to wage war against Canaanite cities in the land (20:16–18), the allowance for meat to be processed and eaten in a nonsacrificial way (12:15–25), and the limitations placed on Israel's future king, lest he rule as an unaccountable tyrant (17:14–20).

Christian Perspective Deuteronomy has had a tremendous impact on Christian thinking from the beginning. Jesus himself quoted it more than any other OT writing, and seventeen of the twenty-seven books of NT make explicit reference to it. The reasons for this are many. For one, Deuteronomy presents one of the clearest messianic prophecies in the OT, the message that another "prophet" like Moses will come and speak the word of God with divine authority (18:15–18). This prophecy is ultimately fulfilled in Jesus Christ (Acts 3:22; 7:37), who grounds his own teaching in the book when he declares that Deuteronomy's call "to love the LORD your God" (6:4) is the greatest commandment of the entire Law (Mt 22:37–38). Likewise, when the devil presses him with temptations, Jesus defends himself with passages from Deuteronomy (6:13, 18; 8:3; Mt 4:4, 7, 10). And when the question of divorce arises, Jesus reveals that Moses only permitted divorce in Deuteronomy on account of the hard hearts of the people (24:1–4; Mt 19:7–8)—a problem that now finds its solution in the grace of the New Covenant, which cleanses the heart (Acts 15:9) and effects a spiritual circumcision of the heart (Rom 2:28–29), just as Moses prophesied in Deuteronomy (30:6). Beyond this, the Song of Moses in 32:1–43 had a far-reaching influence on apostolic teaching related to Christ and the angels, Israel and the Gentiles, and the climactic outcome of salvation history (see Rom 10:19; 15:10; 1 Cor 10:20, 22; Heb 1:6; 10:30; Rev 19:2).

OUTLINE OF DEUTERONOMY

1. Preamble (1:1–5)

2. Historical Prologue (1:6—4:49)
    A. From Horeb to Kadesh (1:6–46)
    B. Wilderness Travel and Conquest (2:1—3:29)
    C. Exhortation to Obedience (4:1–49)

3. Covenant Stipulations (5:1—26:19)
    A. The Decalogue at Horeb (5:1–33)
    B. General Exhortations (6:1—11:32)
    C. Worship and Piety Laws (12:1—16:17)
    D. Civil and Sacred Leadership Laws (16:18—18:22)
    E. Criminal and Judicial Laws (19:1—21:9)
    F. Domestic and Social Laws (21:10—25:19)
    G. Offerings and Commitments (26:1–19)

4. Covenant Sanctions (27:1–30:20)
    A. The Covenant Ceremony (27:1–14)
    B. The Covenant Blessings and Curses (27:15—29:29)
    C. The Future and Final Appeals (30:1–20)

5. Succession Arrangements (31:1–34:12)
    A. The Commission of Joshua (31:1–23)
    B. The Book of the Law (31:24–30)
    C. The Song of Moses (32:1–52)
    D. The Blessings of Moses (33:1–29)
    E. The Death of Moses (34:1–12)

DEUTERONOMY

Events at Horeb Recalled

1 These are the words that Moses spoke to all Israel beyond the Jordan in the wilderness, in the Ar'abah over against Suph, between Par'an and To'phel, La'ban, Haze'roth, and Di'zahab. ²It is eleven days' journey from Horeb by the way of Mount Se'ir to Ka'desh-bar'nea. ³And in the fortieth year, on the first day of the eleventh month, Moses spoke to the sons of Israel according to all that the Lord had given him in commandment to them, ⁴after he had defeated Si'hon the king of the Am'orites, who lived in Heshbon, and Og the king of Bashan, who lived in Ash'taroth and in Ed're-i. ⁵Beyond the Jordan, in the land of Moab, Moses undertook to explain this law, saying, ⁶"The Lord our God said to us in Horeb, 'You have stayed long enough at this mountain; ⁷turn and take your journey, and go to the hill country of the Am'orites, and to all their neighbors in the Ar'abah, in the hill country and in the lowland, and in the Neg'eb, and by the seacoast, the land of the Canaanites, and Lebanon, as far as the great river, the river Euphrates. ⁸Behold, I have set the land before you; go in and take possession of the land which the Lord swore to your fathers, to Abraham, to Isaac, and to Jacob, to give to them and to their descendants after them.'

Appointment of Heads of the Tribes

9 "At that time I said to you, 'I am not able alone to bear you; ¹⁰the Lord your God has multiplied you, and behold, you are this day as the stars of heaven for multitude. ¹¹May the Lord, the God of your fathers, make you a thousand times as many as you are, and bless you, as he has promised you! ¹²How can I bear alone the weight and burden of you and your strife? ¹³Choose wise, understanding, and experienced men, according to your tribes, and I will appoint them as your heads.' ¹⁴And you answered me, 'The thing that you have spoken is good for us to do.' ¹⁵So I took the heads of your tribes, wise and experienced men, and set them as heads over you, commanders of thousands, commanders of hundreds, commanders of fifties, commanders of tens, and officers, throughout your tribes. ¹⁶And I charged your judges at that time, 'Hear the cases between your brethren, and judge righteously between a man and his brother or the alien that is with him. ¹⁷You shall not be partial in judgment; you shall hear the small and the great alike; you shall not be afraid of the face of man, for the judgment is God's; and the case that is too hard for you, you shall bring to me, and I will hear it.' ¹⁸And I commanded you at that time all the things that you should do.

Israel's Refusal to Enter the Land

19 "And we set out from Horeb, and went through all that great and terrible wilderness which you saw, on the way to the hill country of the Am'orites, as the Lord our God commanded us; and

---

1:9–15: Num 11:10–25.   **1:16–18:** Ex 18:25, 26.

1:1 These are the words: An opening formula also used in Hittite vassal treaties of the second millennium B.C. For other parallels between Deuteronomy and these treaties, see introduction: *Structure*, note on 1:31, and word study: *Loved* at 4:37. **Moses spoke:** Deuteronomy presents itself as a record of farewell sermons delivered by Moses shortly before his death (1:5–4:40; 5:1–28:68; 29:2–30:20; 32:1–33:29). **beyond the Jordan:** The setting of the book is east of the Jordan River on the plains of Moab. The Israelites arrived at this destination in Num 22:1.

1:2 Horeb: Another name for Sinai that appears frequently in Deuteronomy (1:6, 19; 4:10, 15; 5:2; 9:8; 18:16; 29:1).

1:3 fortieth year: The final year of the wilderness journey from Egypt to Canaan (2:7). The trip should have lasted less than two years, but the Israelites refused the divine command to seize the Promised Land and thus condemned themselves to wander in the wilderness for another 38 years (2:14; Num

14:34). **eleventh month:** Falls in late winter, two months before Israel crosses the Jordan into Canaan (Josh 4:19).

1:4 Sihon ... Og: Kings of the Transjordan overthrown by the armies of Israel (Num 21:21–35).

1:6—4:49 The historical prologue. It reviews the past relationship between the Lord and Israel in the wilderness, highlighting the faithfulness of God as well as the failings of his people along the way. See introduction: *Structure*.

1:8 the land: The Promised Land, which encompasses Canaan and lower Syria all the way to the Euphrates (1:7; Ex 23:31; Josh 1:4). Israel did not control the full extent of this territory until the kingship of David and Solomon (2 Sam 8:1–14; 1 Kings 4:21, 24). **the Lord swore:** Refers to God's oath to grant the land of Canaan to the patriarchs and their descendants (Gen 15:18–21; 17:8; 26:3; 28:13).

1:9–18 A reference to Ex 18:13–27, where Moses appointed tribal leaders and judges over the people. Lesser disputes were handled in local courts, so that only the more difficult cases came to Moses personally.

1:19–46 A flashback to the events at Kadesh in Num 13–14. It is a painful memory of national rebellion and judgment, when the Exodus generation, paralyzed by fear and unbelief, rejected the Promised Land and excluded itself from its blessings.

1:19 from Horeb: I.e., from Sinai (Num 10:12). **Kadesh-barnea:** In the northeast corner of the Sinai Peninsula. Kadesh

---

The title comes from the mistranslation of 17:18 in the Greek version (the Septuagint) and really means "a second copy of the law." The book comprises the so-called "Deuteronomic Code of Law" (chapters 12–26), edited within the framework of two discourses attributed to Moses represented as prophet and lawgiver. The whole is rounded off with a third discourse, a psalm, and an account of Moses' death and burial. The central theme of Deuteronomy is the election of Israel as the people of God by means of the covenant.

we came to Ka′desh-bar′nea. ²⁰And I said to you, 'You have come to the hill country of the Am′orites, which the LORD our God gives us. ²¹Behold, the LORD your God has set the land before you; go up, take possession, as the LORD, the God of your fathers, has told you; do not fear or be dismayed.' ²²Then all of you came near me, and said, 'Let us send men before us, that they may explore the land for us, and bring us word again of the way by which we must go up and the cities into which we shall come.' ²³The thing seemed good to me, and I took twelve men of you, one man for each tribe; ²⁴and they turned and went up into the hill country, and came to the Valley of Eshcol and spied it out. ²⁵And they took in their hands some of the fruit of the land and brought it down to us, and brought us word again, and said, 'It is a good land which the LORD our God gives us.'

26 "Yet you would not go up, but rebelled against the command of the LORD your God; ²⁷and you murmured in your tents, and said, 'Because the LORD hated us he has brought us forth out of the land of Egypt, to give us into the hand of the Am′orites, to destroy us. ²⁸Where are we going up? Our brethren have made our hearts melt, saying, "The people are greater and taller than we; the cities are great and fortified up to heaven; and moreover we have seen the sons of the An′akim there."' ²⁹Then I said to you, 'Do not be in dread or afraid of them. ³⁰The LORD your God who goes before you will himself fight for you, just as he did for you in Egypt before your eyes, ³¹and in the wilderness, where you have seen how the LORD your God bore you, as a man bears his son, in all the way that you went until you came to this place.' ³²Yet in spite of this word you did not believe the LORD your God, ³³who went before you in the way to seek you out a place to pitch your tents, in fire by night, to show you by what way you should go, and in the cloud by day.

Punishment for Israel's Rebellion

34 "And the LORD heard your words, and was angered, and he swore, ³⁵'Not one of these men of this evil generation shall see the good land which I swore to give to your fathers, ³⁶except Caleb the son of Jephun′neh; he shall see it, and to him and to his children I will give the land upon which he has trodden, because he has wholly followed the LORD!' ³⁷The LORD was angry with me also on your account, and said, 'You also shall not go in there; ³⁸Joshua the son of Nun, who stands before you, he shall enter; encourage him, for he shall cause Israel to inherit it. ³⁹Moreover your little ones, who you said would become a prey, and your children, who this day have no knowledge of good or evil, shall go in there, and to them I will give it, and they shall possess it. ⁴⁰But as for you, turn, and journey into the wilderness in the direction of the Red Sea.'

41 "Then you answered me, 'We have sinned against the LORD; we will go up and fight, just as the LORD our God commanded us.' And every man of you belted on his weapons of war, and thought it easy to go up into the hill country. ⁴²And the LORD said to me, 'Say to them, Do not go up or fight, for I am not in the midst of you; lest you be defeated before your enemies.' ⁴³So I spoke to you, and you would not listen; but you rebelled against the command of the LORD, and were presumptuous and went up into the hill country. ⁴⁴Then the Am′orites who lived in that hill country came out against you and chased you as bees do and beat you down in Se′ir as far as Hormah. ⁴⁵And you returned and wept before the LORD; but the LORD did not listen to your voice or give ear to you. ⁴⁶So you remained at Ka′desh many days, the days that you remained there.

The Years in the Wilderness

2 "Then we turned, and journeyed into the wilderness in the direction of the Red Sea, as the LORD told me; and for many days we went about

---

1:22–46: Num 13:1—14:45; 32:8–13. 1:31: Acts 13:18. 2:1–8: Num 21:4–20.

---

was supposed to be the staging point for Israel's conquest of Canaan in the second year of the Exodus (Num 13:26).

1:22 Let us send men: The people requested spies to gather military intelligence before the invasion of Canaan. Presumably God and Moses endorsed the idea, since both gave commands to this effect (Num 13:1–2, 17).

1:23 twelve men: Listed by name in Num 13:4–16.

1:28 the Anakim: Fearsome warriors in southern Canaan (Num 13:32–33).

1:30 will himself fight for you: Israel is not left to conquer the Promised Land on its own but is assured that God, the divine Warrior, will bring them victory.

1:31 as a man bears his son: The Lord is portrayed as a loving Father carrying his son, Israel, through the wilderness. Several times the book highlights the Fatherhood of God as well as the adoptive sonship of the Israelites (8:5; 14:1; 32:6, 19). This type of kinship language is rooted in the covenant relationship, just as Near Eastern treaties call suzerain kings "fathers" and vassal subjects their "sons" (CCC 238, 441). See note on Ex 4:22.

1:34 he swore: The Lord's oath of disinheritance, which condemned the generation of Israel who escaped Egypt to perish in the wilderness (Num 14:21–35).

1:37 angry with me: Moses, like Israel at Kadesh, was denied entrance into Canaan because of unbelief (Num 14:11; 20:12).

1:39 your little ones: Those who were children when the Exodus generation condemned itself. Persons younger than 20 years old were not eligible for military service (Num 1:3) and so were not held responsible for their parent's refusal to seize the Promised Land (Num 14:29–30). **no knowledge of good or evil:** Refers to the moral innocence of a young child who is unable to distinguish right from wrong (Is 7:16).

1:40 the Red Sea: The Gulf of Aqabah, an inlet of the Red Sea along the east side of the Sinai Peninsula.

2:1—3:11 The final leg of the wilderness journey. At this time, the Israelites avoid conflict with the Edomites (2:1–8), Moabites (2:9–15), and Ammonites (2:16–25) but take up arms against the Amorite kingdoms of Sihon and Og (2:26—3:11). The account is interspersed with historical notes about

Mount Se'ir. ²Then the LORD said to me, ³'You have been going about this mountain country long enough; turn northward. ⁴And command the people, You are about to pass through the territory of your brethren the sons of Esau, who live in Se'ir; and they will be afraid of you. So take good heed; ⁵do not contend with them; for I will not give you any of their land, no, not so much as for the sole of the foot to tread on, because I have given Mount Se'ir to Esau as a possession. ⁶You shall purchase food from them for money, that you may eat; and you shall also buy water of them for money, that you may drink. ⁷For the LORD your God has blessed you in all the work of your hands; he knows your going through this great wilderness; these forty years the LORD your God has been with you; you have lacked nothing.' ⁸So we went on, away from our brethren the sons of Esau who live in Se'ir, away from the Ar'abah road from E'lath and E'zion-ge'ber.

"And we turned and went in the direction of the wilderness of Moab. ⁹And the LORD said to me, 'Do not harass Moab or contend with them in battle, for I will not give you any of their land for a possession, because I have given Ar to the sons of Lot for a possession.' ¹⁰(The E'mim formerly lived there, a people great and many, and tall as the An'akim; ¹¹like the An'akim they are also known as Reph'aim, but the Moabites call them E'mim. ¹²The Horites also lived in Se'ir formerly, but the sons of Esau dispossessed them, and destroyed them from before them, and settled in their stead; as Israel did to the land of their possession, which the LORD gave to them.) ¹³'Now rise up, and go over the brook Ze'red.' So we went over the brook Zered. ¹⁴And the time from our leaving Ka'desh-bar'nea until we crossed the brook Ze'red was thirty-eight years, until the entire generation, that

is, the men of war, had perished from the camp, as the LORD had sworn to them. ¹⁵For indeed the hand of the LORD was against them, to destroy them from the camp, until they had perished.

16 "So when all the men of war had perished and were dead from among the people, ¹⁷the LORD said to me, ¹⁸'This day you are to pass over the boundary of Moab at Ar; ¹⁹and when you approach the frontier of the sons of Ammon, do not harass them or contend with them, for I will not give you any of the land of the sons of Ammon as a possession, because I have given it to the sons of Lot for a possession.' ²⁰(That also is known as a land of Reph'aim; Rephaim formerly lived there, but the Am'monites call them Zamzum'mim, ²¹a people great and many, and tall as the An'akim; but the LORD destroyed them before them; and they dispossessed them, and settled in their stead; ²²as he did for the sons of Esau, who live in Se'ir, when he destroyed the Horites before them, and they dispossessed them, and settled in their stead even to this day. ²³As for the Avvim, who lived in villages as far as Gaza, the Caphtorim, who came from Caphtor, destroyed them and settled in their stead.) ²⁴'Rise up, take your journey, and go over the valley of the Arnon; behold, I have given into your hand Si'hon the Am'orite, king of Heshbon, and his land; begin to take possession, and contend with him in battle. ²⁵This day I will begin to put the dread and fear of you upon the peoples that are under the whole heaven, who shall hear the report of you and shall tremble and be in anguish because of you.'

The Defeat of Sihon the King of Heshbon

26 "So I sent messengers from the wilderness of Ked'emoth to Si'hon the king of Heshbon, with words of peace, saying, ²⁷'Let me pass through your land; I will go only by the road, I will turn aside neither to the right nor to the left. ²⁸You shall sell

---

2:26–37: Num 21:21–32.

---

the displacement of former populations in the region, such as the Emim (by Moab, 2:10–11), the Horites (by Edom, 2:12), and the Zamzummim (by Ammon, 2:20–21). In seizing Amorite lands by force of arms, Israel takes its place among the "conquerors" of the Transjordan.

2:1 Mount Seir: The rugged mountain country south of the Dead Sea. Seir was the name of a Horite chieftain overthrown by the Edomites (2:12; Gen 36:8, 20).

2:4 your brethren: The Edomites are descendants of Esau, and the Israelites are descendants of Esau's twin brother, Jacob (Gen 25:24–26). Hence, the two peoples are kinsfolk.

2:8 we went on, away: The story in Num 20:14–21 indicates that Edom refused to grant Israel safe passage through its territory. **Ezion-geber:** A port at the northern tip of the Gulf of Aqabah (1 Kings 9:26).

2:9 Moab: Southeast of the Dead Sea. Its southern border is the brook Zered, which flows into the lower end of the Dead Sea (2:14), and its northern border at this time was the Arnon valley, which runs into the midpoint of the Dead Sea from the east (2:24). **the sons of Lot:** Both the Moabites and the Ammonites are descendants of Abraham's nephew, Lot (Gen 19:36–37).

2:11 Rephaim: Ancient peoples of the Transjordan remembered for their imposing size and strength (2:10; Gen 14:5). They were also known as the Emim and Zamzummim.

2:14 thirty-eight years: The time elapsed since Israel's apostasy at Kadesh, which occurred in the second year of the Exodus (Num 13–14). Since that time, the Exodus generation that fled slavery in Egypt perished (except Moses, Joshua, and Caleb), while their children, the conquest generation, grew to maturity and made ready to seize the land of Canaan. Israel's journey in the wilderness lasted 40 years total (2:7). See chart: *Chronology of the Exodus* at Num 7. **the LORD had sworn:** The oath of disinheritance and death in Num 14:21–35.

2:19 Ammon: The Ammonites lived northeast of the Moabites.

2:21 the Anakim: See note on 1:28.

2:23 Avvim: A people not otherwise known. **Caphtorim:** One of the "sea peoples" that settled along the southern coastlands of Palestine around 1200 B.C. **Caphtor:** An ancient name for the island of Crete, from whence the Philistines came (Jer 47:4; Amos 9:7).

2:24 Heshbon: Capital of the Amorite kingdom of Sihon in the eastern Transjordan.

me food for money, that I may eat, and give me water for money, that I may drink; only let me pass through on foot, [29]as the sons of Esau who live in Se'ir and the Moabites who live in Ar did for me, until I go over the Jordan into the land which the LORD our God gives to us.' [30]But Si'hon the king of Heshbon would not let us pass by him; for the LORD your God hardened his spirit and made his heart obstinate, that he might give him into your hand, as at this day. [31]And the LORD said to me, 'Behold, I have begun to give Si'hon and his land over to you; begin to take possession, that you may occupy his land.' [32]Then Si'hon came out against us, he and all his people, to battle at Ja'haz. [33]And the LORD our God gave him over to us; and we defeated him and his sons and all his people. [34]And we captured all his cities at that time and utterly destroyed every city, men, women, and children; we left none remaining; [35]only the cattle we took as spoil for ourselves, with the booty of the cities which we captured. [36]From Aro'er, which is on the edge of the valley of the Arnon, and from the city that is in the valley, as far as Gilead, there was not a city too high for us; the LORD our God gave all into our hands. [37]Only to the land of the sons of Ammon you did not draw near, that is, to all the banks of the river Jabbok and the cities of the hill country, and wherever the LORD our God forbade us.

The Defeat of Og the King of Bashan

3 "Then we turned and went up the way to Bashan; and Og the king of Bashan came out against us, he and all his people, to battle at Ed're-i. [2]But the LORD said to me, 'Do not fear him; for I have given him and all his people and his land into your hand; and you shall do to him as you did to Si'hon the king of the Am'orites, who dwelt at Heshbon.' [3]So the LORD our God gave into our hand Og also, the king of Bashan, and all his people; and we struck him until no survivor was left to him. [4]And we took all his cities at that time—there was not a city which

we did not take from them—sixty cities, the whole region of Argob, the kingdom of Og in Bashan. [5]All these were cities fortified with high walls, gates, and bars, besides very many unwalled villages. [6]And we utterly destroyed them, as we did to Si'hon the king of Heshbon, destroying every city, men, women, and children. [7]But all the cattle and the spoil of the cities we took as our booty. [8]So we took the land at that time out of the hand of the two kings of the Am'orites who were beyond the Jordan, from the valley of the Arnon to Mount Hermon [9](the Sido'-nians call Hermon Sir'ion, while the Am'orites call it Se'nir), [10]all the cities of the tableland and all Gilead and all Bashan, as far as Sal'ecah and Ed're-i, cities of the kingdom of Og in Bashan. [11](For only Og the king of Bashan was left of the remnant of the Reph'aim; behold, his bedstead was a bedstead of iron; is it not in Rabbah of the Am'monites? Nine cubits was its length, and four cubits its breadth, according to the common cubit.[a])

12 "When we took possession of this land at that time, I gave to the Reubenites and the Gadites the territory beginning at Aro'er, which is on the edge of the valley of the Arnon, and half the hill country of Gilead with its cities; [13]the rest of Gilead, and all Bashan, the kingdom of Og, that is, all the region of Argob, I gave to the half-tribe of Manas'seh. (The whole of that Bashan is called the land of Reph'aim. [14]Ja'ir the Manas'site took all the region of Argob, that is, Bashan, as far as the border of the Gesh'urites and the Ma-ac'athites, and called the villages after his own name, Hav'voth-ja'ir, as it is to this day.) [15]To Ma'chir I gave Gilead, [16]and to the Reubenites and the Gadites I gave the territory from Gilead as far as the valley of the Arnon, with the middle of the valley as a boundary, as far over as the river Jabbok, the boundary of the Am'monites; [17]the Ar'abah also, with the Jordan as the boundary, from Chin'nereth as far as the sea of the Arabah, the Salt Sea, under the slopes of Pisgah on the east.

3:1–11: Num 21:33–35. **3:12–20:** Num 32.

2:30 God hardened: The Lord brings judgment on Sihon by making him obstinate. He is one of the wicked idolaters who must be cleared away before Israel can settle safely in the land of promise (7:1–5; 9:1–5; 20:16–18). For the mystery of divine hardening in the Exodus story, see note on Ex 4:21.

2:34 utterly destroyed: Means that a wartime ban was in effect requiring Israel to wipe out the entire population of conquered cities. For this military policy, see 20:16–18.

2:37 river Jabbok: A tributary that flows into the Jordan from the east.

3:1 Bashan: The fertile lands east of the Sea of Galilee, rich with forests and pastures (32:14). The snow-covered peak of Mt. Hermon rises at the northern frontier of Bashan.

3:3 no survivor: In compliance with a military ban, as in 2:34.

3:8 Arnon to Mount Hermon: The stretch of land, nearly 150 miles south to north, that Israel conquered under the leadership of Moses (Josh 12:1–6).

3:9 Sirion ... Senir: Names for Mt. Hermon also attested outside the Bible in Canaanite and Assyrian sources.

3:11 Og: The last of the enormous Rephaim that occupied the Transjordan in ancient times. **his bedstead:** Either an actual bed or, as some scholars surmise, a basalt coffin. It measured 13 x 6 feet, had iron framing or fixtures, and was on display for a time in the Ammonite city of Rabbah (modern Amman, capital of Jordan).

3:12–17 Moses partitions the Transjordan into three tribal territories for Reuben (south), Gad (central), and Manasseh (north). The full story is told in Num 32.

3:12 Gilead: The mountain country directly east of the Jordan between Moab and Bashan.

3:17 Chinnereth: The Sea of Galilee region. **the Salt Sea:** The Dead Sea.

---

[a] Heb *cubit of a man.*

18 "And I commanded you at that time, saying, 'The Lord your God has given you this land to possess; all your men of valor shall pass over armed before your brethren the sons of Israel. ¹⁹But your wives, your little ones, and your cattle (I know that you have many cattle) shall remain in the cities which I have given you, ²⁰until the Lord gives rest to your brethren, as to you, and they also occupy the land which the Lord your God gives them beyond the Jordan; then you shall return every man to his possession which I have given you.' ²¹And I commanded Joshua at that time, 'Your eyes have seen all that the Lord your God has done to these two kings; so will the Lord do to all the kingdoms into which you are going over. ²²You shall not fear them; for it is the Lord your God who fights for you.'

Moses Views Canaan from Pisgah

23 "And I begged the Lord at that time, saying, ²⁴'O Lord God, you have only begun to show your servant your greatness and your mighty hand; for what god is there in heaven or on earth who can do such works and mighty acts as yours? ²⁵Let me go over, I pray, and see the good land beyond the Jordan, that excellent hill country, and Lebanon.' ²⁶But the Lord was angry with me on your account, and would not listen to me; and the Lord said to me, 'Let it satisfy you; speak no more to me of this matter. ²⁷Go up to the top of Pisgah, and lift up your eyes westward and northward and southward and eastward, and behold it with your eyes; for you shall not go over this Jordan. ²⁸But charge Joshua, and encourage and strengthen him; for he shall go over at the head of this people, and he shall put them in possession of the land which you shall see.' ²⁹So we remained in the valley opposite Beth-pe'or.

Moses Commands Obedience to God

4 "And now, O Israel, give heed to the statutes and the ordinances which I teach you, and do them; that you may live, and go in and take possession of the land which the Lord, the God of your fathers, gives you. ²You shall not add to the word which I command you, nor take from it; that you may keep the commandments of the Lord your God which I command you. ³Your eyes have seen what the Lord did at Ba'al-pe'or; for the Lord your God destroyed from among you all the men who followed the Ba'al of Peor; ⁴but you who held fast to the Lord your God are all alive this day. ⁵Behold, I have taught you statutes and ordinances, as the Lord my God commanded me, that you should do them in the land which you are entering to take possession of it. ⁶Keep them and do them; for that will be your wisdom and your understanding in the sight of the peoples, who, when they hear all these statutes, will say, 'Surely this great nation is a wise and understanding people.' ⁷For what great nation is there that has a god so near to it as the Lord our God is to us, whenever we call upon him? ⁸And what great nation is there, that has statutes and ordinances so righteous as all this law which I set before you this day?

9 "Only take heed, and keep your soul diligently, lest you forget the things which your eyes have seen, and lest they depart from your heart all the

---

3:23–27: Num 27:12–14; Deut 32:48–52. **4:2:** Rev 22:18, 19. **4:9–14:** Ex 19:1–20, 21.

3:18 pass over armed: Moses required the fighting men of Reuben, Gad, and Manasseh to support the war effort against Canaan (west of the Jordan) before settling with their families in the territories assigned to them (east of the Jordan).

3:21 Joshua: Successor to Moses as leader of Israel (31:7–8). See note on Num 27:18.

3:25 Let me go over: Moses' final plea for permission to enter the Promised Land since being forbidden in Num 20:12. The request is denied, but a small consolation is given: Moses may *see* the land with his eyes, but he may not *enter* the land with the people (3:27).

3:27 Pisgah: Either the slopes or the peak of Mt. Nebo, which rises east of the Jordan across from Jericho (34:1).

3:29 Beth-peor: A shrine in the eastern Jordan valley dedicated to Baal, the storm and fertility god of Canaanite religion. Reference to this location, both here and 4:46, helps to establish the context for Deuteronomy as a whole, bringing to mind how Israel recently committed apostasy at Beth-peor by taking part in idolatry and sexual immorality (4:3; Num 25:1–5). The covenant of Deuteronomy gave Israel an opportunity to renew its broken commitment to the Lord in the aftermath of this national sin.

4:2 You shall not add: Israel is forbidden to tamper with the terms of the covenant. Like other treaties and law codes promulgated in the ancient Near East, Deuteronomy was considered an inviolate document. For a similar warning attached to a NT book, see Rev 22:18–19.

4:3 Baal-peor: Evokes the painful memory of Israel's recent lapse into idolatry in Num 25:1–5. A staggering 24,000 Israelites perished when the Lord sent a plague against the offenders (Num 25:9). See note on 3:29.

4:6 your wisdom: The Torah is a guide to living for the glory of God (Sir 24:23–27). By faithful observance of its precepts, Israel will not only follow the path of wisdom for itself; it will draw the attention of the outside world and move others to admire the righteousness of Israel's God (4:7–8). The moral and spiritual witness of the chosen people will thus have a missionary effect on neighboring nations. For Israel's vocation to the world, see note on Ex 19:6.

4:7 a god so near: The Lord is near to his people in the Torah and the Tabernacle, i.e., in the Law that he gives them and in the sanctuary that is pitched in the center of the Israelite camp (Num 2:1–31).

4:9–14 Moses recalls the manifestation of God's glory on Mt. Horeb (= Sinai), an event witnessed by the generation that came out of Egypt. He remembers how the people heard the Lord speaking the **words** of the Decalogue (4:12; Ex 20:1–7, 22) and how they received further **ordinances** in the Covenant Code (4:14; Ex 21–23). Curiously, Moses speaks as if his audience, the generation of Israelites who were born during the wilderness wandering, **stood at the foot of the mountain**, when in fact it was their parents, now deceased, who were present at Sinai and took part in these events. This way of speaking indicates that the Law is a gift for the whole covenant people spread across time. Beyond this, it points to a developing notion of liturgical "memorial" by which God's saving actions in the past are drawn into the present and made effective for a new generation.

days of your life; make them known to your children and your children's children—¹⁰how on the day that you stood before the Lord your God at Horeb, the Lord said to me, 'Gather the people to me, that I may let them hear my words, so that they may learn to fear me all the days that they live upon the earth, and that they may teach their children so.' ¹¹And you came near and stood at the foot of the mountain, while the mountain burned with fire to the heart of heaven, wrapped in darkness, cloud, and gloom. ¹²Then the Lord spoke to you out of the midst of the fire; you heard the sound of words, but saw no form; there was only a voice. ¹³And he declared to you his covenant, which he commanded you to perform, that is, the ten commandments;ᵇ and he wrote them upon two tables of stone. ¹⁴And the Lord commanded me at that time to teach you statutes and ordinances, that you might do them in the land which you are going over to possess.

15 "Therefore take good heed to yourselves. Since you saw no form on the day that the Lord spoke to you at Horeb out of the midst of the fire, ¹⁶beware lest you act corruptly by making a graven image for yourselves, in the form of any figure, the likeness of male or female, ¹⁷the likeness of any beast that is on the earth, the likeness of any winged bird that flies in the air, ¹⁸the likeness of anything that creeps on the ground, the likeness of any fish that is in the water under the earth. ¹⁹And beware lest you lift up your eyes to heaven, and when you see the sun and the moon and the stars, all the host of heaven, you be drawn away and worship them and serve them, things which the Lord your God has allotted to all the peoples under the whole heaven. ²⁰But the Lord has taken you, and brought you forth out of the iron furnace, out of Egypt, to be a people of his own possession, as at this day. ²¹Furthermore the Lord was angry with me on your account, and he swore that I should not cross the Jordan, and that I should not enter the good land which the Lord your God gives you for an inheritance. ²²For I must die in this land, I must not go over the Jordan; but you shall go over and take possession of that good land. ²³Take heed to yourselves, lest you forget the covenant of the Lord your God, which he made with you, and make a graven image in the form of anything which the Lord your God has forbidden you. ²⁴For the Lord your God is a devouring fire, a jealous God.

25 "When you beget children and children's children, and have grown old in the land, if you act corruptly by making a graven image in the form of anything, and by doing what is evil in the sight of the Lord your God, so as to provoke him to anger, ²⁶I call heaven and earth to witness against you this day, that you will soon utterly perish from the land which you are going over the Jordan to possess; you will not live long upon it, but will be utterly destroyed. ²⁷And the Lord will scatter you among the peoples, and you will be left few in number among the nations where the Lord will drive you. ²⁸And there you will serve gods of wood and stone, the work of men's hands, that neither see, nor hear, nor eat, nor smell. ²⁹But from there you will seek the Lord your God, and you will find him, if you search after him with all your heart and with all your soul. ³⁰When you are in tribulation, and all these things come upon you in the latter days, you will return to the Lord your God and obey his voice, ³¹for the Lord your God is a merciful God; he will not fail you or destroy you or forget the covenant with your fathers which he swore to them.

4:24: Heb 12:29.

4:10 Horeb: Another name for Mt. Sinai.

4:12 saw no form: Because the Lord spoke as a disembodied voice at Sinai, he must not be depicted in the form of any created thing (4:15-24). Imageless worship was required by the first commandment of the Decalogue (Ex 20:1-6) as a way of distinguishing Israelite religion from the cults of the Near East, where idol images abounded and where creation was worshiped instead of the Creator (Rom 1:25). • God, who is spirit, did not assume a physical form until his eternal Son took flesh (Jn 1:14) and became the visible image of the invisible God (Col 1:15) (CCC 2129-31).

4:16 lest you act corruptly: As Israel did by worshiping the golden calf (Ex 32:7-8).

4:19 the host of heaven: The sun, moon, and stars were objects of worship in the religions of the Near East. Even Israel succumbed to this idolatry at times (2 Kings 23:5; Ezek 8:16) (CCC 57). **allotted to all:** The lights of the day and night function as a cosmic clock for the calculation of time (Gen 1:14).

4:20 iron furnace: Used for smelting metals to rid them of impurities. Metaphorically, it refers to the intensity of Israel's suffering back in Egypt (Ex 1:11-14, 22).

4:21 angry with me: The third time Moses mentions this in the book (1:37; 3:26). Only here do we learn that the Lord swore an oath to prevent his entrance into Canaan.

4:24 devouring fire: The Lord burns with divine love, holiness, and jealousy. He renders this mystery concrete by manifesting his presence as fire (e.g., Gen 15:17; Ex 3:2; 19:18) as well as his judgment on sin (e.g., 9:3; Lev 10:1-2; Num 11:1; 16:35). • We must not think that God consumes wood or straw or hay. The God of fire consumes human sins, devouring them and purging them (Origen of Alexandria, *Homilies on Leviticus* 5, 3).

4:25-31 Anticipates in brief what Deut 28-30 prophesies in detail, namely, the future rebellion and restoration of Israel. In covenantal terms, Israel will experience both the curse of exile (4:27) and the blessing of God's mercy that follows (4:31). Idolatry stands out as one of the greatest threats to Israel's continuance in the Promised Land (4:25).

4:26 heaven and earth: Invoked as the witnesses of the Deuteronomic covenant (30:19).

4:30 the latter days: For the meaning of this, see word study: *The Latter Days* at Is 2:2.

ᵇHeb *words.*

32 "For ask now of the days that are past, which were before you, since the day that God created man upon the earth, and ask from one end of heaven to the other, whether such a great thing as this has ever happened or was ever heard of. [33]Did any people ever hear the voice of God speaking out of the midst of the fire, as you have heard, and still live? [34]Or has God ever attempted to go and take a nation for himself from the midst of another nation, by trials, by signs, by wonders, and by war, by a mighty hand and an outstretched arm, and by great terrors, according to all that the LORD your God did for you in Egypt before your eyes? [35]To you it was shown, that you might know that the LORD is God; there is no other besides him. [36]Out of heaven he let you hear his voice, that he might discipline you; and on earth he let you see his great fire, and you heard his words out of the midst of the fire. [37]And because he loved your fathers and chose their descendants after them, and brought you out of Egypt with his own presence, by his great power, [38]driving out before you nations greater and mightier than yourselves, to bring you in, to give you their land for an inheritance, as at this day; [39]know therefore this day, and lay it to your heart, that the LORD is God in heaven above and on the earth beneath; there is no other. [40]Therefore you shall keep his statutes and his commandments, which I command you this day, that it may go well with you, and with your children after you, and that you may prolong your days in the land which the LORD your God gives you for ever."*

Cities of Refuge East of the Jordan

41 †Then Moses set apart three cities in the east beyond the Jordan, [42]that the manslayer might flee there, who kills his neighbor unintentionally, without being at enmity with him in time past, and that by fleeing to one of these cities he might save his life: [43]Bezer in the wilderness on the tableland for the Reubenites, and Ramoth in Gilead for the Gadites, and Golan in Bashan for the Manas'sites.

Moses Sets Forth the Law

44 This is the law which Moses set before the children of Israel; [45]these are the decrees, the statutes, and the ordinances, which Moses spoke to the children of Israel when they came out of Egypt, [46]beyond the Jordan in the valley opposite Beth-pe'or, in the land of Si'hon the king of the Am'orites, who lived at Heshbon, whom Moses and the children of Israel defeated when they came out of Egypt. [47]And they took possession of his land and the land of Og the king of Bashan, the two kings of the Am'orites, who lived to the east beyond the Jordan; [48]from Aro'er, which is on the edge of the valley of the Arnon, as far as Mount Sir'ion[c] (that is, Hermon), [49]together with all the Ar'abah on the east side of the Jordan as far as the Sea of the Arabah, under the slopes of Pisgah.

4:35: Mk 12:32.   **4:41–43:** Num 35:6, 9–34; Deut 19:2–13; Josh 20:7–9.

📖 **4:35 there is no other:** An expression of Israel's monotheistic faith, in which the existence of one god is affirmed and the divinity of pagan idols is denied (4:39; 32:21). It is a claim that the God of Israel is the only deity worthy of the name and that he alone should be worshiped. The existence of "other gods" is still acknowledged, insofar as other nations serve idols that are given names and alleged to have distinct spheres of influence, but not their status as gods and goddesses in the order of being (1 Cor 8:4–6). The basis for this claim is not philosophical reasoning but the experience of the Exodus, an event in which the Lord demonstrated his superiority over the so-called gods of Egypt and brought the nation that worshiped them to its knees (Ex 12:12; 18:11; Num 33:4). • Similar declarations of monotheism appear in the Book of Isaiah (Is 45:5–6, 14, 18, 21–22; 46:9).

4:39 in heaven ... on the earth: Israel's God is the sovereign Lord of all creation, not simply part of creation (Josh 2:11; Ps 139:7–10). This distinguishes him from the gods of other nations, which were associated with forces of nature and were thought to have a limited range of influence.

4:41 three cities: Cities of refuge east of the Jordan. See note on Josh 20:1–9.

4:48 Sirion: The Sidonian name for Mt. Hermon (3:9).

4:49 Sea of the Arabah: The Dead Sea.

*4:32–40: This passage gives the clearest and most eloquent expression of Israel's consciousness of its election as the people of God.
†4:41: The beginning of the second discourse of Moses containing the Deuteronomic version of the Ten Commandments; cf. Ex 20:1–17.
[c]Syr: Heb *Sion.*

Word Study

Loved (4:37)

'Ahab (Heb.): the verb "to love", used variously in the OT to denote parental love (Gen 22:2), spousal love (Gen 24:67), neighborly love (Lev 19:18), friendly love (1 Sam 18:1), and a devout love for the Lord (Ex 20:6). Love is a key theme in Deuteronomy, where it is always covenantal rather than sentimental. It is an expression of loyalty to the Lord and obedience to his covenant (Deut 5:10; 10:12–13; 30:20). In this respect, as in others, Deuteronomy parallels Near Eastern vassal treaties, in which "love" is a technical term for the obligations laid upon covenant parties. A suzerain king swears to love his vassal by pledging to offer protection, and a vassal swears to love the king in the form of exclusive loyalty and faithful observance of the treaty stipulations. In Deuteronomy, the Lord is the king who declares his love for Israel (Deut 7:12–13; 23:5), while the Israelites are commanded to love the Lord by obedience to his covenant (Deut 6:5; 11:1; 30:16) (CCC 218–19).

The Ten Commandments

5 And Moses summoned all Israel, and said to them, "Hear, O Israel, the statutes and the ordinances which I speak in your hearing this day, and you shall learn them and be careful to do them. ²The LORD our God made a covenant with us in Horeb. ³Not with our fathers did the LORD make this covenant, but with us, who are all of us here alive this day. ⁴The LORD spoke with you face to face at the mountain, out of the midst of the fire, ⁵while I stood between the LORD and you at that time, to declare to you the word of the LORD; for you were afraid because of the fire, and you did not go up into the mountain. He said:

6 " 'I am the LORD your God, who brought you out of the land of Egypt, out of the house of bondage.

7 " 'You shall have no other gods before[d] me.

8 You shall not make for yourself a graven image, or any likeness of anything that is in heaven above, or that is on the earth beneath, or that is in the water under the earth; ⁹you shall not bow down to them or serve them; for I the LORD your

---

5:6–21: Ex 20:2–17.

5:1—26:19 The central chapters of Deuteronomy set forth the covenant stipulations that Israel is bound to observe. General stipulations appear in chaps. 5–11 and specific stipulations follow in chaps. 12–26. See introduction: *Structure*.

5:3 our fathers: The patriarchs Abraham, Isaac, and Jacob (1:8; 6:10).

5:4 face to face: Directly, i.e., apart from the mediation of Moses. This applies to the Decalogue (4:10–13) but not to the rest of the Sinai covenant (4:14).

5:5 I stood between: Moses was a mediator of divine revelation to Israel. He was elected to this role (Ex 20:19) after the Lord uttered the Ten Commandments from Mt. Sinai (Ex 20:1–17, 22). All laws given subsequent to the Decalogue were relayed to the people through Moses (Ex 21–23; 25–31; 34:10–28; Lev 1:1–2, etc.). **afraid:** For Israel's fear, see Ex 20:18.

5:6–21 The Ten Commandments, also listed in Ex 20:1–17. The two versions are substantially the same, except that **(1)** Deuteronomy offers a different motive for keeping the Sabbath than Exodus (compare 5:15 with Ex 20:11), and **(2)** the ninth and tenth commandments in Exodus appear in reverse order in Deuteronomy (compare 5:21 with Ex 20:17). Traditional catechesis, following St. Augustine, adopts the order of the commandments in Deuteronomy (CCC 2066). For commentary on the precepts of the Decalogue, see notes on Ex 20:1–17.

5:9–10 The Lord's anger, which extends for three or four generations, is outmatched by his merciful love, which pours out for thousands.

ᵈOr *besides*.

What Is a Covenant?

Nearly every aspect of biblical life and religion revolves around "covenant". This is hardly surprising, since covenants were cornerstones of social, political, and religious life in the ancient Near East. The covenant motif in the Bible is no less pervasive and ultimately far more important. Why? Because covenants draw us into a relationship with God. Covenants thus function as the driving force behind salvation history.

Covenant Membership

Covenants are formal agreements between two parties that are sealed by oath. In the biblical world, covenants create bonds of kinship between persons who are unrelated by extending the rights and responsibilities of family membership to persons outside the family. They make it possible for non-relatives to become the equivalent of flesh-and-blood relatives. Unlike contracts, which establish temporary relationships for the purpose of doing business, covenants establish permanent relationships that enlarge one's family. Persons who are bound together by covenant are thus described in kinship terms ("father", "son", "brother", etc.); likewise, the obligations that attach to these relationships are described as kinship commitments ("love", "loyalty", "faithfulness", etc.). Rather than a mechanical exchange of goods and services, which is the purpose of a contract, a covenant is a mutual exchange of persons who pledge themselves to one another. This is captured in Scripture in what is called the "covenant formula", which states: "I ... will be your God, and you shall be my people" (Lev 26:12; cf. Ezek 37:27; Hos 2:23; Zech 13:9; 2 Cor 6:16; Rev 21:3). Marriage and adoption are the two institutions in our modern experience that best illustrate the notion of kinship by covenant as it functioned in the biblical world (cf. Ps 2:7; 2 Sam 7:14; Ezek 16:8; Mal 2:14).

Covenant Making

Formal procedures were necessary to ratify a covenant and make it binding. Swearing an oath is central and indispensable, since without an oath a covenant cannot exist. Oaths are taken by one or both parties who pledge themselves to commitments or "stipulations" set forth in advance. In every oath, the Lord (or "the gods" in ancient Near East treaties) is called upon to witness the covenant and to enforce its terms by meting out its rewards and punishments. This means that God makes himself responsible for sending blessings upon faithful oath-takers and curses upon faithless oath-breakers. A covenant oath is typically a verbal pledge that calls upon the name of the Lord and places the one who swears it under a conditional self-curse (cf. Josh 2:19; Ruth 1:17; Mk 14:71). Sometimes the verbal formula is reinforced by a ritual and liturgical enactment of the oath. Symbolic oath rites include offering sacrifice (Ps 50:5), sharing a meal (Gen 31:44–55; Ex 24:8–11), raising a hand to heaven (Deut 32:40; Rev 10:5–6), walking between divided animals (Gen

God am a jealous God, visiting the iniquity of the fathers upon the children to the third and fourth generation of those who hate me, [10]but showing merciful love to thousands of those who love me and keep my commandments.

11 "'You shall not take the name of the LORD your God in vain: for the LORD will not hold him guiltless who takes his name in vain.

12 "'Observe the sabbath day, to keep it holy, as the LORD your God commanded you. [13]Six days you shall labor, and do all your work; [14]but the seventh day is a sabbath to the LORD your God; in it you shall not do any work, you, or your son, or your daughter, or your manservant, or your maidservant, or your ox, or your donkey, or any of your cattle, or the sojourner who is within your gates, that your manservant and your maidservant may rest as well as you. [15]You shall remember that you were a servant in the land of Egypt, and the LORD your God brought you out from there with a mighty hand and an outstretched arm; therefore the LORD your God commanded you to keep the sabbath day.

16 "'Honor your father and your mother, as the LORD your God commanded you; that your days may be prolonged, and that it may go well with you, in the land which the LORD your God gives you.

17 "'You shall not kill.

18 "'Neither shall you commit adultery.

19 "'Neither shall you steal.

20 "'Neither shall you bear false witness against your neighbor.

21 "'Neither shall you covet your neighbor's wife; and you shall not desire your neighbor's house, his field, or his manservant, or his maidservant, his ox, or his donkey, or anything that is your neighbor's.'

Moses the Mediator of God's Will

22 "These words the LORD spoke to all your assembly at the mountain out of the midst of the fire, the cloud, and the thick darkness, with a loud voice;

5:14: Ex 20:8–11; 23:12.   5:16–20: Mt 19:18, 19; Mk 10:19; Lk 18:20.   5:16: Mt 15:4; Mk 7:10; Eph 6:3.
5:17, 18: Jas 2:11.   5:17–21: Rom 13:9.   5:18: Mt 5:27; Rom 7:7.   5:21: Rom 7:7.   5:22–27: Ex 20:18–21.

5:15 God brought you out: The Sabbath, like the Exodus, is intended to be a liberating event. Laying aside work every seventh day memorializes how Israel left behind the toil of Egypt for the Lord's gift of freedom (CCC 2170).

5:22 spoke ... wrote: The Lord gave the commandments audibly at first (Ex 20:1–17) and then in writing (Ex 24:12) (CCC 2056, 2059). **added no more:** The significance of this statement is twofold: it means **(1)** that God no longer spoke to Israel directly

---

15:7–21; Jer 34:18), and placing a hand under the thigh (Gen 24:2–9; 47:29). Gestures such as sharing a meal symbolize the *blessing* of peace that unites the covenant parties, while actions involving sacrifice and death often symbolize the *curse* that will fall upon one who breaks the covenant.

Covenant Models

Covenants could assume different forms depending upon their function. Classifications are not rigid, but three types can be distinguished. **(1)** A *kinship covenant* is a covenant between individuals or groups of relatively equal rank. On this model, both parties swear an oath and both parties assume obligations toward one another. Bilateral covenants of kinship often take the form of peace treaties, or covenants of nonaggression, such as those between Jacob and Laban (Gen 31:44–54) and David and Jonathan (1 Sam 18:3; 20:8, 42). **(2)** A *treaty covenant* is a covenant between partners of unequal rank. These were frequently made when a superior such as a suzerain king imposed an oath of allegiance upon an inferior such as a vassal king. Examples of treaty covenants in Scripture include the covenant of circumcision made with Abraham and his descendants (Gen 17:1–21) and the Deuteronomic covenant made with Israel on the plains of Moab (Deut 1–34). **(3)** A *grant covenant* is also a covenant made between partners of unequal rank, usually a suzerain king and his vassal. Unlike a treaty covenant, however, which requires obedience from a subordinate, a covenant of grant rewards the obedience of a subordinate. Kings in biblical times swore oaths to reward vassals for exceptional loyalty by granting them (and their descendants) such things as a dynasty or tract of land. A grant covenant is a unilateral arrangement in which a superior pledges an inheritable gift to an inferior. Conditions may have been attached in some cases, but a covenant of grant was typically an unconditional arrangement. Examples of grant covenants in Scripture include the pledge of the Promised Land to Abraham's family (Gen 15:18–21), the pledge to bless all nations through Abraham's offspring (Gen 22:16–18), the pledge of a perpetual priestly line to Phinehas (Num 25:10–13), and the pledge of an everlasting throne and kingdom to David and his successors on the throne (2 Sam 7:11–17; Ps 89:3–4; 132:11–12).

Covenants in Scripture, though they follow conventional models and procedures of the biblical world, are nevertheless unique. Covenants between individuals and nations in Semitic antiquity invoked gods and goddesses as witnesses and enforcers of the covenant, but never as partners in the covenant. The Bible, by contrast, presents us with divine covenants in which the Lord acts as a full partner in forging kinship relations with his people. No other known religion, ancient or modern, holds that God has sworn oaths to make us part of his family. Yet this is the marvelous truth of the Bible. God is a divine Father who adopts us as his children and unites us with himself in an everlasting bond of loyalty and love.

and he added no more. And he wrote them upon two tables of stone, and gave them to me. ²³And when you heard the voice out of the midst of the darkness, while the mountain was burning with fire, you came near to me, all the heads of your tribes, and your elders; ²⁴and you said, 'Behold, the Lᴏʀᴅ our God has shown us his glory and greatness, and we have heard his voice out of the midst of the fire; we have this day seen God speak with man and man still live. ²⁵Now therefore why should we die? For this great fire will consume us; if we hear the voice of the Lᴏʀᴅ our God any more, we shall die. ²⁶For who is there of all flesh, that has heard the voice of the living God speaking out of the midst of fire, as we have, and has still lived? ²⁷Go near, and hear all that the Lᴏʀᴅ our God will say; and speak to us all that the Lᴏʀᴅ our God will speak to you; and we will hear and do it.'

28 "And the Lᴏʀᴅ heard your words, when you spoke to me; and the Lᴏʀᴅ said to me, 'I have heard the words of this people, which they have spoken to you; they have rightly said all that they have spoken. ²⁹Oh that they had such a mind as this always, to fear me and to keep all my commandments, that it might go well with them and with their children for ever! ³⁰Go and say to them, "Return to your tents." ³¹But you, stand here by me, and I will tell you all the commandment and the statutes and the ordinances which you shall teach them, that they may do them in the land which I give them to possess.' ³²You

shall be careful to do therefore as the Lᴏʀᴅ your God has commanded you; you shall not turn aside to the right hand or to the left. ³³You shall walk in all the way which the Lᴏʀᴅ your God has commanded you, that you may live, and that it may go well with you, and that you may live long in the land which you shall possess.

The Great Commandment

6 "Now this is the commandment, the statutes and the ordinances which the Lᴏʀᴅ your God commanded me to teach you, that you may do them in the land to which you are going over, to possess it; ²that you may fear the Lᴏʀᴅ your God, you and your son and your son's son, by keeping all his statutes and his commandments, which I command you, all the days of your life; and that your days may be prolonged. ³Hear therefore, O Israel, and be careful to do them; that it may go well with you, and that you may multiply greatly, as the Lᴏʀᴅ, the God of your fathers, has promised you, in a land flowing with milk and honey.

4 *"Hear, O Israel: The Lᴏʀᴅ our God is one Lᴏʀᴅ;ᵉ ⁵and you shall love the Lᴏʀᴅ your God with all your heart, and with all your soul, and with all your might. ⁶And these words which I command you this day shall be upon your heart; ⁷and you shall teach them diligently to your children, and shall talk of them when you sit in your house, and when you walk by the way, and when you lie down, and when

---

6:4, 5: Mt 22:37; Mk 12:29, 30; Lk 10:27.   **6:6–9:** Deut 6:20–25; 11:18–20.

---

after he uttered the Decalogue and **(2)** that the Decalogue is the heart of the Sinai covenant, all other laws being applications (Ex 21–23) or legislative additions to this central core (e.g., the sacrificial laws of Leviticus were not part of the original Sinai covenant, Jer 7:22–23). For legal amendments made to the Sinai covenant, see essay: *After the Golden Calf* at Ex 34.

5:27 we will hear and do: Israel promised to live by the Sinai laws in Ex 19:8 and then swore an oath to do so in Ex 24:3, 7. This pledge is renewed at Shechem after Israel's conquest of the Promised Land (Josh 24:1–28).

5:28–33 The Lord ratifies the election of Moses as a mediator and lawgiver.

5:33 that you may live: Obedience is a path to national security and prosperity for Israel, i.e., it will bring the people a long and blessed life in Canaan. Disobedience, by contrast, will result in dispersion and exile from the land (4:25–27; 28:62–64).

6:1 the commandment: The love command of 6:4–5. **statutes ... ordinances:** The stipulations of the covenant spelled out in chaps. 12–26.

6:4 Hear, O Israel: A solemn address used several times in the book (5:1; 6:3; 9:1). It introduces the Shema of 6:4–9, named after the Hebrew term translated "hear" (*shema*'). Devout Jews have recited this prayer twice

a day since ancient times. **The Lᴏʀᴅ our God is one Lᴏʀᴅ:** A confession of faith in the Lord's oneness and uniqueness. The statement affirms **(1)** that Israel believes and serves only one God and **(2)** that Israel's God is not merely the highest god in a pantheon of deities but is without equal, in a class by himself. In this way, Israel's faith is defined over against the polytheistic religions of the ancient world. For more on monotheism, see note on 4:35. • The NT affirms the oneness of God revealed in the OT (Jn 17:3; 1 Tim 2:5) but expands this belief with the additional revelation of three Divine Persons existing within the oneness of God (Mt 28:19; Jn 1:1; 10:30; 15:26; 2 Cor 13:14). The Christian doctrine of the Trinity is thus a deepening of OT revelation rather than a departure from it (CCC 200-202). • We say that the Father, Son, and Spirit are one God in a unity of nature. But we dare not say that the Person of the Father is the same as the Son or the Spirit, or that the Person of the Son is the Father or the Spirit, or that the Person of the Spirit is the Father or the Son (St. Fulgentius, *On the Faith* 1, 3).

6:5 love the Lᴏʀᴅ: With the full powers of one's mind and will. An emotional sentiment is not in view. See word study: *Loved* at 4:37. • Jesus declared this law to be the first and greatest precept of the Mosaic Law (Mt 22:36-38) (CCC 2083).

6:6 upon your heart: A call to internalize God's Law so that it shapes one's entire life from the inside out (Ps 37:31; Prov 3:3).

6:7 your children: The family is a school of religious instruction. Responsibility for the spiritual formation of children thus rests with parents, whom the Lord has tasked with transmitting the faith to the next generation (4:9; 11:19; Eph 6:4).

---

*6:4–9: The recital thrice daily of this text, plus two others, is the principal practice of piety of the religious Jew; it is called the Shema ("Hear"). It contains the greatest commandment of the Law, that is, the love of the covenant-God (cf. Mt 22:37), and a clear statement of monotheism.

ᵉOr *the Lᴏʀᴅ our God, the Lᴏʀᴅ is one*. Or *the Lᴏʀᴅ is our God, the Lᴏʀᴅ is one*. Or *the Lᴏʀᴅ is our God, the Lᴏʀᴅ alone*.

you rise. ⁸And you shall bind them as a sign upon your hand, and they shall be as frontlets between your eyes. ⁹And you shall write them on the doorposts of your house and on your gates.

Caution against Disobedience

10 "And when the LORD your God brings you into the land which he swore to your fathers, to Abraham, to Isaac, and to Jacob, to give you, with great and excellent cities, which you did not build, ¹¹and houses full of all good things, which you did not fill, and cisterns hewn out, which you did not hew, and vineyards and olive trees, which you did not plant, and when you eat and are full, ¹²then take heed lest you forget the LORD, who brought you out of the land of Egypt, out of the house of bondage. ¹³You shall fear the LORD your God; you shall serve him, and swear by his name. ¹⁴You shall not go after other gods, of the gods of the peoples who are round about you; ¹⁵for the LORD your God in the midst of you is a jealous God; lest the anger of the LORD your God be kindled against you, and he destroy you from off the face of the earth.

16 "You shall not put the LORD your God to the test, as you tested him at Massah. ¹⁷You shall diligently keep the commandments of the LORD your God, and his decrees, and his statutes, which he has commanded you. ¹⁸And you shall do what is right and good in the sight of the LORD, that it may go well with you, and that you may go in and take possession of the good land which the LORD swore to give to your fathers ¹⁹by thrusting out all your enemies from before you, as the LORD has promised.

20 "When your son asks you in time to come, 'What is the meaning of the decrees and the statutes and the ordinances which the LORD our God has commanded you?' ²¹then you shall say to your son, 'We were Pharaoh's slaves in Egypt; and the LORD brought us out of Egypt with a mighty hand; ²²and the LORD showed signs and wonders, great and grievous, against Egypt and against Pharaoh and all his household, before our eyes; ²³and he brought us out from there, that he might bring us in and give us the land which he swore to give to our fathers. ²⁴And the LORD commanded us to do all these statutes, to fear the LORD our God, for our good always, that he might preserve us alive, as at this day. ²⁵And it will be righteousness for us, if we are careful to do all this commandment before the LORD our God, as he has commanded us.'

A Chosen People

7 "When the LORD your God brings you into the land which you are entering to take possession of it, and clears away many nations before you, the Hittites, the Gir′gashites, the Am′orites, the Canaanites, the Per′izzites, the Hi′vites, and the Jeb′usites, seven nations greater and mightier than yourselves, ²and when the LORD your God gives them over to you, and you defeat them; then you must utterly destroy them; you shall make no covenant with them, and show no mercy to them. ³You shall not make marriages with them, giving your daughters to their sons or taking their daughters for your sons. ⁴For they would turn away your sons from following me, to serve other gods; then the anger of the LORD would be kindled against you, and he would destroy you quickly. ⁵But thus shall you deal with them: you shall break down their altars, and dash in pieces their pillars, and hew down their Ashe′rim, and burn their graven images with fire.

6:8: Ex 13:9, 16; Deut 11:18. **6:13:** Mt 4:10; Lk 4:8. **6:16:** Mt 4:7; Lk 4:12. **7:1:** Acts 13:19.
7:2-4: Ex 23:32, 33; 34:12, 15, 16. **7:3:** Ex 34:15, 16. **7:5:** Ex 23:24; 34:13; Num 33:52; Deut 12:3.

6:8-9 Inspired the Jewish tradition of making "phylacteries" and "mezuzot". Phylacteries are small boxes containing Scripture verses that are strapped to the left arm and forehead during prayer (11:18). Mezuzot are small receptacles with Scripture verses fixed to the doorframe of the home (11:20).

6:10 you did not build: Envisions an Israelite takeover of Canaanite cities and settlements. As a matter of military policy, the battle for the Promised Land will focus on eliminating enemy inhabitants while leaving their property intact. Only three cities in Canaan will be leveled and burned: Jericho, Ai, and Hazor (Josh 6:24; 8:28; 11:13).

6:13 you shall serve him: The Lord alone must be the object of Israel's allegiance and worship (CCC 2084, 2096). See word study: *Serve* at Ex 4:23. • Jesus invokes this verse when he repels the wilderness temptation to worship the devil (Mt 4:10).

6:16 You shall not ... test: A warning not to repeat the mistake of Ex 17:1-7, where Israel questioned the Lord's goodness and accused him of hostile intent in leading the people into the wilderness. • Jesus defends himself with this verse when the devil challenges him to jump from the Temple and test God's promise of protection (Mt 4:7) (CCC 2119).

6:25 righteousness: Conformity to the standards of the covenant, which is attained by faithful obedience to the Lord's commandments (24:13; Ps 106:31; Is 48:18; Lk 1:6).

7:1-5 Israelites must maintain a complete separation from Canaanites. Associations with them are forbidden at political (no covenants, 7:2), social (no intermarriage, 7:3), and religious levels (no idolatry, 7:5).

7:1 seven nations: The peoples who lived in Canaan prior to its conquest by the Israelites. The number is either abbreviated or symbolizes "totality", since the Pentateuch elsewhere counts as many as ten nations occupying the Promised Land (Gen 15:18-21). See note on Ex 3:8.

7:2 utterly destroy: A military ban that mandates the total destruction of an enemy and forbids the confiscation of spoils (20:16-18). For the rationale behind this extreme policy, see essay: *The Conquest of Canaan* at Josh 6.

7:3 not make marriages: Mixed marriages threaten the purity of Israel's faith and life. Failure to heed this warning will lead many away from the Lord into idolatry (see Judg 3:5-6; 1 Kings 11:1-8; Ps 106:34-39).

7:5 Asherim: The word is plural, referring to sacred trees or poles dedicated to Asherah, a fertility goddess of the Canaanite religion. The Lord demands demolition of all such cultic

6 "For you are a people holy to the Lord your God; the Lord your God has chosen you to be a people for his own possession, out of all the peoples that are on the face of the earth. ⁷It was not because you were more in number than any other people that the Lord set his love upon you and chose you, for you were the fewest of all peoples; ⁸but it is because the Lord loves you, and is keeping the oath which he swore to your fathers, that the Lord has brought you out with a mighty hand, and redeemed you from the house of bondage, from the hand of Pharaoh king of Egypt. ⁹Know therefore that the Lord your God is God, the faithful God who keeps covenant and merciful love with those who love him and keep his commandments, to a thousand generations, ¹⁰and repays to their face those who hate him, by destroying them; he will not be slack with him who hates him, he will repay him to his face. ¹¹You shall therefore be careful to do the commandment, and the statutes, and the ordinances, which I command you this day.

Blessing for Obedience

12 "And because you listen to these ordinances, and keep and do them, the Lord your God will keep with you the covenant and the merciful love which he swore to your fathers to keep; ¹³he will love you, bless you, and multiply you; he will also bless the fruit of your body and the fruit of your ground, your grain and your wine and your oil, the increase of your cattle and the young of your flock, in the land which he swore to your fathers to give you. ¹⁴You shall be blessed above all peoples; there shall not be male or female barren among you, or among your cattle. ¹⁵And the Lord will take away from you all sickness; and none of the evil diseases of Egypt, which you knew, will he inflict upon you, but he will lay them upon all who hate you. ¹⁶And you shall destroy all the peoples that the Lord your God will give over to you, your eye shall not pity them; neither shall you serve their gods, for that would be a snare to you.

17 "If you say in your heart, 'These nations are greater than I; how can I dispossess them?' ¹⁸you shall not be afraid of them, but you shall remember what the Lord your God did to Pharaoh and to all Egypt, ¹⁹the great trials which your eyes saw, the signs, the wonders, the mighty hand, and the outstretched arm, by which the Lord your God brought you out; so will the Lord your God do to all the peoples of whom you are afraid. ²⁰Moreover the Lord your God will send hornets among them, until those who are left and hide themselves from you are destroyed. ²¹You shall not be in dread of them; for the Lord your God is in the midst of you, a great and terrible God. ²²The Lord your God will clear away these nations before you little by little; you may not make an end of them at once, ᶠ lest the wild beasts grow too numerous for you. ²³But the Lord your God will give them over to you, and throw them into great confusion, until they are destroyed. ²⁴And he will give their kings into your hand, and you shall make their name perish from under heaven; not a man shall be able to stand against you, until you have destroyed them. ²⁵The graven images of

---

7:6: Ex 19:5; 22:31; Lev 11:44, 45; 19:2; 20:7, 26; Num 15:40; Deut 14:2, 21; 26:19; 28:9.

---

objects (12:2–3; Ex 34:13–16). **burn their graven images:** Just as Moses had done with the golden calf idol (9:21; Ex 32:20).

7:6–8 Moses expounds the theology of Israel's election. The divine choice to set Israel apart as a holy nation is an unmerited grace. It is based, not on Israel's greatness or worthiness, but on God's love and loyalty expressed in his covenant with the family of Abraham. In the economy of salvation, the election of one nation as God's people was a means to a greater end, namely, the redemption of all peoples in the messianic age (Is 49:6; Jn 4:22) (CCC 218, 762). See notes on 4:6 and Ex 19:6.

7:8 redeemed: Purchased and set free by a ransom price.

7:12–16 Obedience to the covenant will bring God's blessings upon families, flocks, and fields as well as protection from sickness and disease. These are outlined in more detail in 28:1–14.

7:22 little by little: The conquest of Canaan, here described as a gradual process, is elsewhere envisioned as a rapid process (9:3). Both predictions are true: the initial conquests will be quick and decisive, while a complete settlement of the land will be a long and drawn-out endeavor.

7:25 graven images: Idols are placed under a ban, meaning they must be destroyed (7:5), while their precious metals must be purified by fire (Num 31:21–23) and devoted to the Lord in the sanctuary (Josh 6:19).

ᶠ Or *quickly.*

Word Study

Possession (7:6)

Segullah (Heb.) means "property", often with the connotation of something highly valued and carefully guarded. As a secular term, it can refer to the royal treasures of a king (1 Chron 29:3; Eccles 2:8). As a theological term, it describes Israel as a people elected and loved by the Lord. Israel is God's treasured possession, the people he cherishes and protects as uniquely his own (Ex 19:5; Deut 14:2; Ps 135:4). Later in the OT, when a time of judgment becomes necessary, the Lord promises to single out a faithful remnant within Israel as his special possession (Mal 3:17). The idea of a *segullah* carries over into the NT as a description of the messianic People of God in Tit 2:14 and 1 Pet 2:9.

their gods you shall burn with fire; you shall not covet the silver or the gold that is on them, or take it for yourselves, lest you be ensnared by it; for it is an abomination to the LORD your God. ²⁶And you shall not bring an abominable thing into your house, and become accursed like it; you shall utterly detest and abhor it; for it is an accursed thing.

A Warning Not to Forget God

8 "All the commandment which I command you this day you shall be careful to do, that you may live and multiply, and go in and possess the land which the LORD swore to give to your fathers. ²And you shall remember all the way which the LORD your God has led you these forty years in the wilderness, that he might humble you, testing you to know what was in your heart, whether you would keep his commandments, or not. ³And he humbled you and let you hunger and fed you with manna, which you did not know, nor did your fathers know; that he might make you know that man does not live by bread alone, but that man lives by everything that proceeds out of the mouth of the LORD. ⁴Your clothing did not wear out upon you, and your foot did not swell, these forty years. ⁵Know then in your heart that, as a man disciplines his son, the LORD your God disciplines you. ⁶So you shall keep the commandments of the LORD your God, by walking in his ways and by fearing him. ⁷For the LORD your God is bringing you into a good land, a land of brooks of water, of fountains and springs, flowing forth in valleys and hills, ⁸a land of wheat and barley, of vines and fig trees and pomegranates, a land of olive trees and honey, ⁹a land in which you will eat bread without scarcity, in which you will lack nothing, a land whose stones are iron, and out of whose hills you can dig copper. ¹⁰And you shall eat and be full, and you shall bless the LORD your God for the good land he has given you.

11 "Take heed lest you forget the LORD your God, by not keeping his commandments and his ordinances and his statutes, which I command you this day: ¹²lest, when you have eaten and are full, and have built excellent houses and live in them, ¹³and when your herds and flocks multiply, and your silver and gold is multiplied, and all that you have is multiplied, ¹⁴then your heart be lifted up, and you forget the LORD your God, who brought you out of the land of Egypt, out of the house of bondage, ¹⁵who led you through the great and terrible wilderness, with its fiery serpents and scorpions and thirsty ground where there was no water, who brought you water out of the flinty rock, ¹⁶who fed you in the wilderness with manna which your fathers did not know, that he might humble you and test you, to do you good in the end. ¹⁷Beware lest you say in your heart, 'My power and the might of my hand have gotten me this wealth.' ¹⁸You shall remember the LORD your God, for it is he who gives you power to get wealth; that he may confirm his covenant which he swore to your fathers, as at this day. ¹⁹And if you forget the LORD your God and go after other gods and serve them and worship them, I solemnly warn you this day that you shall surely perish. ²⁰Like the nations that the LORD makes to perish before you, so shall you perish, because you would not obey the voice of the LORD your God.

Consequences of Rebelling against God

9 "Hear, O Israel; you are to pass over the Jordan this day, to go in to dispossess nations greater and mightier than yourselves, cities great and fortified up to heaven, ²a people great and tall, the sons of the An'akim, whom you know, and of whom you have heard it said, 'Who can stand before the sons of A'nak?' ³Know therefore this day that he who goes over before you as a devouring fire is the LORD your God; he will destroy them and subdue them before you; so you shall drive them out, and make them perish quickly, as the LORD has promised you.

8:3: Mt 4:4; Lk 4:4. **9:3**: Heb 12:29.

8:2 forty years: The duration of the wilderness period between Israel's departure from Egypt and its entrance into Canaan. For the symbolism of the number, see Num 14:32-34 and note on Lk 4:2. **testing you:** Just as the Lord tested the faith and fidelity of Abraham (Gen 22:1-2).

8:3 manna: The bread from heaven that sustained Israel during its long journey through the wilderness (Ex 16:35). Daily provisions of manna expressed God's loving care for the needs of his people. See note on Ex 16:4. **by bread alone:** The miracle of the manna taught Israel that people have spiritual needs in addition to material needs. Ignorance of the word of God starves the human spirit just as hunger weakens the body (CCC 1334). • Jesus rebukes Satan with this verse when the devil tries to divert him from the Father's plan (Mt 4:4).

8:4 did not wear out: The preservation of clothing is yet another Exodus miracle (29:5).

8:5 as a man disciplines his son: The Lord is a Father who trains his people in righteousness by correcting their mis-

behavior (4:36; 11:1-2). Discipline, although unpleasant, is a sure sign of his paternal love (Prov 3:12; Heb 12:7-11). Among other things, it is meant to induce humility (8:2, 16), so that the People of God will not become prideful and trust in themselves (8:17). The father-son relationship between the Lord and Israel arises from the covenant bond that unites them. See note on 1:31.

8:7-10 Besides flowing with "milk and honey" (6:3), Canaan abounds with natural resources that make prosperity in the ancient world possible (land, water, food, metals).

8:14 your heart be lifted up: Refers to a prideful sense of self-accomplishment. The danger, here and in 8:17-18, is that Israel will mistake grace for works, thinking that a prosperous life in Canaan will be their own doing and not the gift of God (Ps 44:1-3; Eph 2:8-9).

9:2 the Anakim: Fearsome warriors in southern Canaan (Num 13:32-33).

4 "Do not say in your heart, after the Lord your God has thrust them out before you, 'It is because of my righteousness that the Lord has brought me in to possess this land'; whereas it is because of the wickedness of these nations that the Lord is driving them out before you. ⁵Not because of your righteousness or the uprightness of your heart are you going in to possess their land; but because of the wickedness of these nations the Lord your God is driving them out from before you, and that he may confirm the word which the Lord swore to your fathers, to Abraham, to Isaac, and to Jacob.

6 "Know therefore, that the Lord your God is not giving you this good land to possess because of your righteousness; for you are a stubborn people. ⁷Remember and do not forget how you provoked the Lord your God to wrath in the wilderness; from the day you came out of the land of Egypt, until you came to this place, you have been rebellious against the Lord. ⁸Even at Horeb you provoked the Lord to wrath, and the Lord was so angry with you that he was ready to destroy you. ⁹When I went up the mountain to receive the tables of stone, the tables of the covenant which the Lord made with you, I remained on the mountain forty days and forty nights; I neither ate bread nor drank water. ¹⁰And the Lord gave me the two tables of stone written with the finger of God; and on them were all the words which the Lord had spoken with you on the mountain out of the midst of the fire on the day of the assembly. ¹¹And at the end of forty days and forty nights the Lord gave me the two tables of stone, the tables of the covenant. ¹²Then the Lord said to me, 'Arise, go down quickly from here; for your people whom you have brought from Egypt have acted corruptly; they have turned aside quickly out of the way which I commanded them; they have made themselves a molten image.'

13 "Furthermore the Lord said to me, 'I have seen this people, and behold, it is a stubborn people; ¹⁴let me alone, that I may destroy them and blot out their name from under heaven; and I will make of you a nation mightier and greater than they.' ¹⁵So I turned and came down from the mountain, and the mountain was burning with fire; and the two tables of the covenant were in my two hands. ¹⁶And I looked, and behold, you had sinned against the Lord your God; you had made yourselves a molten calf; you had turned aside quickly from the way which the Lord had commanded you. ¹⁷So I took hold of the two tables, and cast them out of my two hands, and broke them before your eyes. ¹⁸Then I lay prostrate before the Lord as before, forty days and forty nights; I neither ate bread nor drank water, because of all the sin which you had committed, in doing what was evil in the sight of the Lord, to provoke him to anger. ¹⁹For I was afraid of the anger and hot displeasure which the Lord bore against you, so that he was ready to destroy you. But the Lord listened to me that time also. ²⁰And the Lord was so angry with Aaron that he was ready to destroy him; and I prayed for Aaron also at the same time. ²¹Then I took the sinful thing, the calf which you had made, and burned it with fire and crushed it, grinding it very small, until it was as fine as dust; and I threw the dust of it into the brook that descended out of the mountain.

22 "At Tab′erah also, and at Massah, and at Kib′roth-hatta′avah, you provoked the Lord to wrath. ²³And when the Lord sent you from Ka′desh-bar′nea, saying, 'Go up and take possession of the land which I have given you,' then you rebelled against the commandment of the Lord your God, and did not believe him or obey his voice. ²⁴You have been rebellious against the Lord from the day that I knew you.

9:8–21: Ex 32:7–20.

9:4 my righteousness: A plea for humility. Possession of the land of Canaan will be an unmerited grace that rebellious Israel neither deserves nor can claim as its own achievement. It is based rather on (1) the wickedness of the Canaanites, who are about to face judgment for their iniquities (Gen 15:16), and (2) the faithfulness of God, who swore an oath to grant the land of Canaan to the family of Abraham (9:5; Gen 15:18-21; 17:8). See essay: *The Conquest of Canaan* at Josh 6. • *Morally*, when we achieve success in warring against the vices of the flesh and have gained freedom from the world's way of life, let us not be puffed up with the success, believing the victory came through our own efforts. You would never have prevailed without the Lord helping, strengthening, and protecting you (St. John Cassian, *Conferences* 5, 15).

9:6—10:11 A flashback on two critical events at the start of the wilderness period: the *breaking* of the Sinai covenant, effected by the worship of the golden calf (9:8-21), and the *renewal* of the Sinai covenant, symbolized by the reissuing of the Decalogue on a new set of tablets, the elevation of the

Levites to sacred ministry, and the Lord's response of mercy to the intercession of Moses (9:25–10:11). For the background, see Ex 32-34.

9:8 at Horeb: I.e., at Mt. Sinai.

9:9 up the mountain: Moses climbed to the summit of Mt. Sinai and spent forty days with the Lord soon after the covenant was first ratified (Ex 24:15-18). When he finally came down, he was enraged to find Israel worshiping the golden calf (9:15-17; Ex 32:15-20).

9:18 I lay prostrate: In prayerful intercession for sinful Israel (9:25-29). forty days ... forty nights: Moses spent another forty days on Sinai after the golden calf apostasy (9:9; Ex 24:18).

9:22-23 Sites associated with Israel's wilderness rebellions. Besides the apostasy at Sinai, the people complained at **Taberah** (Num 11:1-3); they clamored for water and made accusations against the Lord at **Massah** (Ex 17:1-7); they demanded meat instead of manna at **Kibroth-hattaavah** (Num 11:4-6, 31-35); and they refused to heed the Lord's command to seize the Promised Land at **Kadesh-barnea** (Num 14).

25 "So I lay prostrate before the Lord for these forty days and forty nights, because the Lord had said he would destroy you. 26And I prayed to the Lord, 'O Lord God, do not destroy your people and your heritage, whom you have redeemed through your greatness, whom you have brought out of Egypt with a mighty hand. 27Remember your servants, Abraham, Isaac, and Jacob; do not regard the stubbornness of this people, or their wickedness, or their sin, 28lest the land from which you brought us say, "Because the Lord was not able to bring them into the land which he promised them, and because he hated them, he has brought them out to slay them in the wilderness." 29For they are your people and your heritage, whom you brought out by your great power and by your outstretched arm.'

The Second Pair of Stone Tables

10 "At that time the Lord said to me, 'Hew two tables of stone like the first, and come up to me on the mountain, and make an ark of wood. 2And I will write on the tables the words that were on the first tables which you broke, and you shall put them in the ark.' 3So I made an ark of acacia wood, and hewed two tables of stone like the first, and went up the mountain with the two tables in my hand. 4And he wrote on the tables, as at the first writing, the ten commandments*g* which the Lord had spoken to you on the mountain out of the midst of the fire on the day of the assembly; and the Lord gave them to me. 5Then I turned and came down from the mountain, and put the tables in the ark which I had made; and there they are, as the Lord commanded me.

6 "(The sons of Israel journeyed from Be-er'-oth Be'ne-ja'akan*h* to Mose'rah. There Aaron died, and

there he was buried; and his son Elea'zar ministered as priest in his stead. 7From there they journeyed to Gud'godah, and from Gudgodah to Jot'bathah, a land with brooks of water. 8At that time the Lord set apart the tribe of Levi to carry the ark of the covenant of the Lord, to stand before the Lord to minister to him and to bless in his name, to this day. 9Therefore Levi has no portion or inheritance with his brothers; the Lord is his inheritance, as the Lord your God said to him.)

10 "I stayed on the mountain, as at the first time, forty days and forty nights, and the Lord listened to me that time also; the Lord was unwilling to destroy you. 11And the Lord said to me, 'Arise, go on your journey at the head of the people, that they may go in and possess the land, which I swore to their fathers to give them.'

The Essence of the Law

12 "And now, Israel, what does the Lord your God require of you, but to fear the Lord your God, to walk in all his ways, to love him, to serve the Lord your God with all your heart and with all your soul, 13and to keep the commandments and statutes of the Lord, which I command you this day for your good? 14Behold, to the Lord your God belong heaven and the heaven of heavens, the earth with all that is in it; 15yet the Lord set his heart in love upon your fathers and chose their descendants after them, you above all peoples, as at this day. 16Circumcise therefore the foreskin of your heart, and be no longer stubborn. 17For the Lord your God is God of gods and Lord of lords, the great, the mighty, and the terrible God, who is not partial and takes no bribe. 18He executes justice for the fatherless and

---

9:25–29: Ex 32:11–14.   **10:17:** Acts 10:34; Gal 2:6; Rev 17:14; 19:16.

9:28 lest the land ... say: I.e., lest the annihilation of Israel send the wrong message to the Egyptians, namely, that the Lord is weak in the face of the Canaanites and hateful toward his own people.

10:1 At that time: The time when the broken Sinai covenant was being renewed with Moses in Ex 34:1–28. **two tables:** A second set of tablets was inscribed with the Ten Commandments (Ex 34:1) to replace the first set shattered by Moses (Ex 32:19). See note on Ex 31:18.

10:3 ark: Used for storage of the Ten Commandments. See note on Ex 25:10.

10:6–7 A parenthetical aside that jumps from the *first* year of the Exodus at Sinai to the *fortieth* year of the Exodus in the wilderness. Part of the travel itinerary parallels the list in Num 33:31, and Eleazar's succession to the high priesthood of Aaron summarizes the story in Num 20:22–29.

10:8 At that time: Resumes the Sinai narrative of 10:1 after the brief aside of 10:6–7. **carry the ark:** The Levites were tasked with transporting the Tabernacle and its furnishings through the wilderness (Num 1:50). The clan of Kohath was responsible for carrying the ark (Num 3:29–31). **to minister ...**

to bless: The Levitical family of Aaron was ordained to priestly ministry (Ex 40:12–15) and charged with blessing the people (Num 6:22–27).

10:9 no portion: The tribe of Levi will receive no land inheritance in Canaan. See word study: *Inheritance* at Josh 13:7.

10:14 the heaven of heavens: A superlative expression, meaning "the highest heaven" (1 Kings 8:27).

10:16 Circumcise ... your heart: Circumcision is an outward sign of an inward act. Removing the foreskin of the flesh symbolizes the need to cut away the stubbornness of the human heart and consecrate it to the Lord through obedience (Jer 4:4). To have an uncircumcised heart is to be unresponsive to God and unfaithful to the demands of his covenant (Jer 9:25–26). See word study: *Heart* at 30:6.

10:17 Lord of lords: A superlative expression, meaning "the highest Lord". Given the covenant framework of Deuteronomy, it means that Israel owes its highest allegiance to the Lord over every other god and sovereign. For use of this title in the NT, see Rev 19:16. **not partial:** The Lord is a just Judge who shows no favoritism and accepts no bribes (16:19–20; Gen 18:25).

10:18 fatherless ... widow: Deuteronomy expresses humanitarian concern for the weak and vulnerable. Its laws appeal to the compassion of the Lord himself (14:28–29; 15:7–11, 13–15; 24:19–21; 26:12).

---

g Heb *words.*
h Or *the wells of the Bene-jaakan.*

the widow, and loves the sojourner, giving him food and clothing. ¹⁹Love the sojourner therefore; for you were sojourners in the land of Egypt. ²⁰You shall fear the LORD your God; you shall serve him and cling to him, and by his name you shall swear. ²¹He is your praise; he is your God, who has done for you these great and terrible things which your eyes have seen. ²²Your fathers went down to Egypt seventy persons; and now the LORD your God has made you as the stars of heaven for multitude.

Rewards for Obedience

11 "You shall therefore love the LORD your God, and keep his charge, his statutes, his ordinances, and his commandments always. ²And consider this day (since I am not speaking to your children who have not known or seen it), consider the discipline ᶦ of the LORD your God, his greatness, his mighty hand and his outstretched arm, ³his signs and his deeds which he did in Egypt to Pharaoh the king of Egypt and to all his land; ⁴and what he did to the army of Egypt, to their horses and to their chariots; how he made the water of the Red Sea overflow them as they pursued after you, and how the LORD has destroyed them to this day; ⁵and what he did to you in the wilderness, until you came to this place; ⁶and what he did to Da'than and Abi'ram the sons of Eli'ab, son of Reuben; how the earth opened its mouth and swallowed them up, with their households, their tents, and every living thing that followed them, in the midst of all Israel; ⁷for your eyes have seen all the great work of the LORD which he did.

8 "You shall therefore keep all the commandment which I command you this day, that you may be strong, and go in and take possession of the land which you are going over to possess, ⁹and that you may live long in the land which the LORD swore to your fathers to give to them and to their descendants, a land flowing with milk and honey. ¹⁰For the land which you are entering to take possession of it is not like the land of Egypt, from which you have come, where you sowed your seed and watered it with your feet, like a garden of vegetables; ¹¹but the land which you are going over to possess is a land of hills and valleys, which drinks water by the rain from heaven, ¹²a land which the LORD your God cares for; the eyes of the LORD your God are always upon it, from the beginning of the year to the end of the year.

13 "And if you will obey my commandments which I command you this day, to love the LORD your God, and to serve him with all your heart and with all your soul, ¹⁴heʲ will give the rain for your land in its season, the early rain and the later rain, that you may gather in your grain and your wine and your oil. ¹⁵And heʲ will give grass in your fields for your cattle, and you shall eat and be full. ¹⁶Take heed lest your heart be deceived, and you turn aside and serve other gods and worship them, ¹⁷and the anger of the LORD be kindled against you, and he shut up the heavens, so that there be no rain, and the land yield no fruit, and you perish quickly off the good land which the LORD gives you.

18 "You shall therefore lay up these words of mine in your heart and in your soul; and you shall bind them as a sign upon your hand, and they shall be as frontlets between your eyes. ¹⁹And you shall teach them to your children, talking of them when you are sitting in your house, and when you are walking by the way, and when you lie down, and when you rise. ²⁰And you shall write them upon the doorposts of your house and upon your gates, ²¹that your days and the days of your children may be multiplied in the land which the LORD swore to your fathers to give them, as long as the heavens are above the earth. ²²For if you will be careful to do all this commandment which I command you to do, loving the LORD your God, walking in all his ways, and clinging to him, ²³then the LORD will drive out all these nations before you, and you will dispossess nations greater and mightier than yourselves. ²⁴Every place on which the sole of your foot treads shall be yours; your territory shall be from the

---

10:19: Ex 22:21; 23:9; Lev 19:34. **10:22:** Acts 7:14.

10:21 your praise: I.e., the object of Israel's praise (Ps 22:3; 109:1).

10:22 seventy persons: The size of Jacob's family that migrated to Egypt from the land of Canaan (Gen 46:26–27). **as the stars:** Recalls the promise made to Abraham (Gen 15:5). Israel grew into a mighty nation by the time of the Exodus (Ex 12:37).

11:1 love the LORD: The primary obligation of the Deuteronomic covenant. See word study: *Loved* at 4:37.

11:6 Dathan and Abiram: Two rebels from the tribe of Reuben who challenged the authority of Moses (Num 16:12–14) and perished when the earth opened beneath them (Num 16:25–30).

11:10 watered it: The farmlands of Egypt were irrigated by Israelite slaves. Such toilsome labor will not be necessary in Canaan, which receives from the Lord a blessed abundance of seasonal rainfall (11:11).

11:14 the rain: The early rains in Palestine come in the fall (October-November), and the late rains come in the spring (March-April). Crops are sown in the fall, and the harvest season stretches from spring (wheat, barley) to late summer (grapes, olives). • *Allegorically,* rain is the preaching that waters the world. The Lord gave the early rain when, in former times, he gave his people knowledge of the Law. He gave the latter rain when, in the last days, he proclaimed the mystery of his Incarnation through the Church (St. Gregory the Great, *Moralia on Job* 20, 2).

11:18–21 On the popular piety inspired by these commands, see note on 6:8–9.

11:24 your territory: The Promised Land encompasses all of Canaan and lower Syria. See note on Josh 1:4. **the western sea:** The Mediterranean Sea.

ᶦ Or *instruction.*
ʲ Sam Gk Vg: Heb *I.*

wilderness and Lebanon and from the River, the river Euphrates, to the western sea. [25]No man shall be able to stand against you; the LORD your God will lay the fear of you and the dread of you upon all the land that you shall tread, as he promised you.

26 "Behold, I set before you this day a blessing and a curse: [27]the blessing, if you obey the commandments of the LORD your God, which I command you this day, [28]and the curse, if you do not obey the commandments of the LORD your God, but turn aside from the way which I command you this day, to go after other gods which you have not known. [29]And when the LORD your God brings you into the land which you are entering to take possession of it, you shall set the blessing on Mount Ger′izim and the curse on Mount E′bal. [30]Are they not beyond the Jordan, west of the road, toward the going down of the sun, in the land of the Canaanites who live in the Ar′abah, over against Gilgal, beside the Oak[k] of Mo′reh? [31]For you are to pass over the Jordan to go in to take possession of the land which the LORD your God gives you; and when you possess it and live in it, [32]you shall be careful to do all the statutes and the ordinances which I set before you this day.

Pagan Shrines to Be Destroyed

12 "These are the statutes and ordinances which you shall be careful to do in the land which the LORD, the God of your fathers, has given you to possess, all the days that you live upon the earth. [2]*You shall surely destroy all the places where the nations whom you shall dispossess served their gods, upon the high mountains and upon the hills and under every green tree; [3]you shall tear down their altars, and dash in pieces their pillars, and burn their Ashe′rim with fire; you shall hew down the graven images of their gods, and destroy their name out of that place. [4]You shall not do so to the LORD your God. [5]But you shall seek the place which the LORD your God will choose out of all your tribes to put his name and make his habitation there; there you shall go, [6]and there you shall bring your burnt offerings and your sacrifices, your tithes and the offering that you present, your votive offerings, your freewill offerings, and the firstlings of your herd and of your flock; [7]and there you shall eat before the LORD your God, and you shall rejoice, you and your households, in all that you undertake, in which the LORD your God has blessed you. [8]You shall not do according to all that we are doing here this day, every man doing whatever is right in his own eyes; [9]for you have not as yet come to the rest and to the inheritance which the LORD your God gives you. [10]But when you go over the Jordan, and live in the land which the LORD your God gives you to inherit, and when he gives you rest from all your enemies round about, so that you live in safety, [11]then to the place which the LORD your God will choose, to make his name dwell there, there you shall bring all that I command you: your burnt offerings and your sacrifices, your tithes and the offering that you present, and all your votive offerings which you vow to the LORD. [12]And you shall rejoice before the LORD your God, you and your sons and your daughters, your menservants and your maidservants, and the Levite that is within your towns, since he has no portion or inheritance with you. [13]Take heed that you do not offer your burnt offerings at every place that you

---

12:1–28: Ex 20:24.

11:26 a blessing and a curse: The covenant sanctions, which are spelled out in 28:1-68.

11:29-32 The ratification ceremony for the Deuteronomic covenant. It will take place on twin mountains, **Gerizim** and **Ebal**, that overlook the city of Shechem in central Canaan. The liturgy is described in 27:1-26 and enacted in Josh 8:30-35.

11:30 Oak of Moreh: A landmark near Shechem. Abraham consecrated this site when he built an altar to the Lord under the tree on his arrival in Canaan (Gen 12:6-7).

12:1–26:19 Chaps. 12-26 set forth *specific* stipulations of the covenant, just as chaps. 5-11 outline the *general* stipulations of the covenant. In doing so, Deuteronomy follows the pattern of a Near Eastern vassal treaty. See introduction: *Structure.*

12:2 destroy: Mandates a religious crusade against idolatry, one that calls for a full suppression of Canaan's pagan cults and a complete demolition of its cultic sites and objects (7:5).

12:3 pillars: Large stones propped upright as idol monuments. Israel is forbidden to erect them (16:22). **Asherim:** Sacred poles or trees. See note on 7:5.

12:5 the place: The law of the central sanctuary. It points to a future time, after war gives way to peace, when the Lord will select a permanent location for his dwelling in Israel (12:10). This is the only site where the Israelites will be permitted to worship the Lord in sacrifice (12:11). The purpose of the law is **(1)** to promote the *unity* of Israel's tribes as a worshiping community and **(2)** to guard the *purity* of Israel's faith from Canaanite idolatry. Centralizing worship at a single sanctuary thus fosters national solidarity and gives the Levitical clergy tight control over liturgical practice, lest deviant forms of worship spring up in the land where priestly oversight is lacking. Note that selecting a single "place" for sacrifice stands in contrast to the many "places" of Canaanite worship in the land (12:2). Notice, too, that the "place" of the central sanctuary is unspecified in Deuteronomy. Not until the reigns of David and Solomon does God reveal that Jerusalem is the chosen location (1 Kings 8:15-21; 1 Chron 22:1; 2 Chron 6:6). **his name:** An idiom for God's presence among his people. This does not mean Deuteronomy naïvely confines his presence to the sanctuary, since it recognizes that the Lord also dwells in the highest heaven (26:15).

12:8 right in his own eyes: I.e., as each person sees fit.

12:13 not ... at every place: A revision of earlier legislation in Ex 20:24 that will go into effect when the site for the central sanctuary is chosen (12:11). Centuries later, the prophet Malachi envisions a lifting of this restriction when he foresees the worldwide worship of messianic times (Mal 1:11).

---

*12:2: This law, enforcing one single place of worship, connects historically with the religious reform of Josiah just before the Exile in the opinion of many scholars; cf. 2 Kings 22–23.

[k]Gk Syr: See Gen 12:6. Heb *Oaks* or *Terebinths.*

see; ¹⁴but at the place which the LORD will choose in one of your tribes, there you shall offer your burnt offerings, and there you shall do all that I am commanding you.

Concerning Eating

15 "However, you may slaughter and eat flesh within any of your towns, as much as you desire, according to the blessing of the LORD your God which he has given you; the unclean and the clean may eat of it, as of the gazelle and as of the deer. ¹⁶Only you shall not eat the blood; you shall pour it out upon the earth like water. ¹⁷You may not eat within your towns the tithe of your grain or of your wine or of your oil, or the firstlings of your herd or of your flock, or any of your votive offerings which you vow, or your freewill offerings, or the offering that you present; ¹⁸but you shall eat them before the LORD your God in the place which the LORD your God will choose, you and your son and your daughter, your manservant and your maidservant, and the Levite who is within your towns; and you shall rejoice before the LORD your God in all that you undertake. ¹⁹Take heed that you do not forsake the Levite as long as you live in your land.

20 "When the LORD your God enlarges your territory, as he has promised you, and you say, 'I will eat flesh,' because you crave flesh, you may eat as much flesh as you desire. ²¹If the place which the LORD your God will choose to put his name there is too far from you, then you may kill any of your herd or your flock, which the LORD has given you, as I have commanded you; and you may eat within your towns as much as you desire. ²²Just as the gazelle or the deer is eaten, so you may eat of it; the unclean and the clean alike may eat of it. ²³Only be sure that you do not eat the blood; for the blood is the life, and you shall not eat the life with the flesh.

²⁴You shall not eat it; you shall pour it out upon the earth like water. ²⁵You shall not eat it; that all may go well with you and with your children after you, when you do what is right in the sight of the LORD. ²⁶But the holy things which are due from you, and your votive offerings, you shall take, and you shall go to the place which the LORD will choose, ²⁷and offer your burnt offerings, the flesh and the blood, on the altar of the LORD your God; the blood of your sacrifices shall be poured out on the altar of the LORD your God, but the flesh you may eat. ²⁸Be careful to heed all these words which I command you, that it may go well with you and with your children after you for ever, when you do what is good and right in the sight of the LORD your God.

Warning against Idolatry

29 "When the LORD your God cuts off before you the nations whom you go in to dispossess, and you dispossess them and dwell in their land, ³⁰take heed that you be not ensnared to follow them, after they have been destroyed before you, and that you do not inquire about their gods, saying, 'How did these nations serve their gods?—that I also may do likewise.' ³¹You shall not do so to the LORD your God; for every abominable thing which the LORD hates they have done for their gods; for they even burn their sons and their daughters in the fire to their gods.

³²¹"Everything that I command you you shall be careful to do; you shall not add to it or take from it.

13 "If a prophet arises among you, or a dreamer of dreams, and gives you a sign or a wonder, ²and the sign or wonder which he tells you comes to pass, and if he says, 'Let us go after other gods,' which you have not known, 'and let us serve them,' ³you shall not listen to the words of that prophet or to that dreamer of dreams; for the LORD your God

---

12:16, 23: Lev 17:10–14; 19:26. **12:29–32:** Ex 23:24; 34:12–14; Num 33:52.

12:15 slaughter and eat flesh: Profane slaughter is permitted, a revision of earlier legislation in Lev 17:3-6, which stipulates that animals killed for food must be sacrificed at the Tabernacle before being eaten. Now that Israel's tribes are about to enter Canaan and disperse throughout the land, with many living at great distances from the sanctuary, the Levitical law is impractical, and so permission is given to process meat in a non-sacrificial way. In Deuteronomy, then, one may slaughter animals *any* place, but one may sacrifice animals only at *one* place (12:13-14). **as of the gazelle:** Cattle, sheep, and goats may be slaughtered and eaten like game animals taken in hunting. The one exception is unblemished firstlings, which must be sacrificed to the Lord at the sanctuary (15:19-23).

12:16 not eat the blood: Reaffirms the Levitical ban on blood consumption (Lev 17:11).

12:17 may not eat: Foods and animals that are dedicated to the Lord must still be sacrificed at the central sanctuary before their consumable portions may be eaten (12:18, 26-27).

12:31 burn their sons: Canaanites sacrificed children by fire to the god Molech (Lev 18:21), a homicidal ritual that ensnared even Israelites at times (2 Kings 3:27; Ezek 20:31).

12:32 you shall not add: The stipulations of the covenant are not subject to amendment. See note on 4:2.

13:1-18 Laws to counteract the spread of idolatry in Israel. Instigators of this crime, whether false prophets, family members, or friends, must be handed over to public execution promptly and without pity (13:5, 9). Towns that forsake the Lord for other gods are likewise doomed to destruction (13:15). Idolatry is a capital offense because it constitutes high treason against the Lord of the covenant.

13:1 a dreamer: A false prophet who claims to have received divine revelation through dreams (Jer 23:25). See word study: *Dream* at Gen 37:5.

13:2 go after other gods: One test of a true prophet is orthodox theology. Another is his ability to forecast future events with accuracy (18:22).

13:3 God is testing: A test of one's faithfulness to God's word (8:2; Gen 22:1). • According to Deuteronomy, if a teacher of the Church wanders from the faith, Divine Providence

---

¹ Ch 13:1 in Heb.

is testing you, to know whether you love the LORD your God with all your heart and with all your soul. [4]You shall walk after the LORD your God and fear him, and keep his commandments and obey his voice, and you shall serve him and cling to him. [5]But that prophet or that dreamer of dreams shall be put to death, because he has taught rebellion against the LORD your God, who brought you out of the land of Egypt and redeemed you out of the house of bondage, to make you leave the way in which the LORD your God commanded you to walk. So you shall purge the evil from the midst of you.

6 "If your brother, the son of your mother, or your son, or your daughter, or the wife of your bosom, or your friend who is as your own soul, entices you secretly, saying, 'Let us go and serve other gods,' which neither you nor your fathers have known, [7]some of the gods of the peoples that are round about you, whether near you or far off from you, from the one end of the earth to the other, [8]you shall not yield to him or listen to him, nor shall your eye pity him, nor shall you spare him, nor shall you conceal him; [9]but you shall kill him; your hand shall be first against him to put him to death, and afterwards the hand of all the people. [10]You shall stone him to death with stones, because he sought to draw you away from the LORD your God, who brought you out of the land of Egypt, out of the house of bondage. [11]And all Israel shall hear, and fear, and never again do any such wickedness as this among you.

12 "If you hear in one of your cities, which the LORD your God gives you to dwell there, [13]that certain base fellows have gone out among you and have drawn away the inhabitants of the city, saying, 'Let us go and serve other gods,' which you have not known, [14]then you shall inquire and make search and ask diligently; and behold, if it be true

and certain that such an abominable thing has been done among you, [15]you shall surely put the inhabitants of that city to the sword, destroying it utterly, all who are in it and its cattle, with the edge of the sword. [16]You shall gather all its spoil into the midst of its open square, and burn the city and all its spoil with fire, as a whole burnt offering to the LORD your God; it shall be a heap for ever, it shall not be built again. [17]None of the devoted things shall cling to your hand; that the LORD may turn from the fierceness of his anger, and show you mercy, and have compassion on you, and multiply you, as he swore to your fathers, [18]if you obey the voice of the LORD your God, keeping all his commandments which I command you this day, and doing what is right in the sight of the LORD your God.

Pagan Practices Forbidden

14 "You are the sons of the LORD your God; you shall not cut yourselves or make any baldness on your foreheads for the dead. [2]For you are a people holy to the LORD your God, and the LORD has chosen you to be a people for his own possession, out of all the peoples that are on the face of the earth.

3 "You shall not eat any abominable thing. [4]These are the animals you may eat: the ox, the sheep, the goat, [5]the deer, the gazelle, the roebuck, the wild goat, the ibex, the antelope, and the mountain-sheep. [6]Every animal that parts the hoof and has the hoof cloven in two, and chews the cud, among the animals, you may eat. [7]Yet of those that chew the cud or have the hoof cloven you shall not eat these: The camel, the hare, and the rock badger, because they chew the cud but do not part the hoof, are unclean for you. [8]And the swine, because it parts the hoof but does not chew the cud, is unclean for you. Their flesh you shall not eat, and their carcasses you shall not touch.

14:1: Lev 19:28.   **14:2:** Ex 19:5, 6; Deut 26:19; Tit 2:14; 1 Pet 2:9; Rev 1:6; 5:10.   **14:3–20:** Lev 11:2–23.

---

permits this in order to test our love for God. A true and genuine Catholic is one who loves the truth of God, the Church, and the Body of Christ (St. Vincent of Lérins, *The Commonitory* 19–20).

13:5 put to death: The only law in the Torah that prescribes the death penalty for heresy.

13:9 first: The informant must be the first to hurl stones at the offender.

13:11 hear, and fear: Public executions serve as deterrents to further criminal mischief.

13:13 base fellows: Literally "sons of Belial". Later Jewish writings use the term "Belial" as an epithet for Satan. An alternative form, Beliar, appears with this meaning in the Greek text of 2 Cor 6:15.

13:16 whole burnt offering: The military operation has a cultic dimension, i.e., the destruction of wickedness is akin to a sacrifice offered to the Lord (Lev 1:3–9). **a heap:** The town must lie in perpetual ruins (Josh 8:28).

13:17 devoted things: Things dedicated to the Lord and banned from personal confiscation. A complete ban is placed on all persons and property found in apostate cities, lest the

desire for gain compromise the investigation of the facts. See word study: *Devoted* at Josh 6:17.

14:1 sons of the LORD: The adoptive sonship of Israel is rooted in its covenant bond with the Lord, the divine Father (32:6). See note on 1:31. **cut ... baldness:** Self-laceration and shaving the head are pagan mourning rituals (Jer 41:5; Amos 8:10).

14:2 holy: Set apart from other nations to serve the Lord in a special way (Lev 20:26). **his own possession:** A reference to Israel's election as God's people. See note on 7:6–8 and word study: *Possession* at 7:6.

14:3–21 Reiterates the Mosaic dietary laws of Lev 11:1–47, where distinctions between clean and unclean foods are set forth in greater detail.

14:3 the ox, the sheep, the goat: Sacrificial animals. Unlike Leviticus, Deuteronomy mentions them specifically because it authorizes the slaughter of these animals throughout the land apart from the Lord's sanctuary. Their consumption is now a dietary issue in local settings. See note on 12:15.

14:6 parts the hoof: I.e., has hoofs for feet rather than paws or claws.

9 "Of all that are in the waters you may eat these: Whatever has fins and scales you may eat. [10]And whatever does not have fins and scales you shall not eat; it is unclean for you.

11 "You may eat all clean birds. [12]But these are the ones which you shall not eat: the eagle, the vulture, the osprey, [13]the buzzard, the kite, after their kinds; [14]every raven after its kind; [15]the ostrich, the nighthawk, the sea gull, the hawk, after their kinds; [16]the little owl and the great owl, the water hen [17]and the pelican, the carrion vulture and the cormorant, [18]the stork, the heron, after their kinds; the hoopoe and the bat. [19]And all winged insects are unclean for you; they shall not be eaten. [20]All clean winged things you may eat.

21 "You shall not eat anything that dies of itself; you may give it to the alien who is within your towns, that he may eat it, or you may sell it to a foreigner; for you are a people holy to the LORD your God.

"You shall not boil a kid in its mother's milk.

Regulations concerning Tithes

22 "You shall tithe all the yield of your seed, which comes forth from the field year by year. [23]And before the LORD your God, in the place which he will choose, to make his name dwell there, you shall eat the tithe of your grain, of your wine, and of your oil, and the firstlings of your herd and flock; that you may learn to fear the LORD your God always. [24]And if the way is too long for you, so that you are not able to bring the tithe, when the LORD your God blesses you, because the place is too far from you, which the LORD your God chooses, to set his name there, [25]then you shall turn it into money, and bind up the money in your hand, and go to the place which the LORD your God chooses, [26]and spend the money for whatever you desire, oxen, or sheep, or wine or strong drink, whatever your appetite craves; and you shall eat

there before the LORD your God and rejoice, you and your household. [27]And you shall not forsake the Levite who is within your towns, for he has no portion or inheritance with you.

28 "At the end of every three years you shall bring forth all the tithe of your produce in the same year, and lay it up within your towns; [29]and the Levite, because he has no portion or inheritance with you, and the sojourner, the fatherless, and the widow, who are within your towns, shall come and eat and be filled; that the LORD your God may bless you in all the work of your hands that you do.

Concerning the Sabbatical Year

15 At the end of every seven years you shall grant a release. [2]And this is the manner of the release: every creditor shall release what he has lent to his neighbor; he shall not exact it of his neighbor, his brother, because the LORD's release has been proclaimed. [3]Of a foreigner you may exact it; but whatever of yours is with your brother your hand shall release. [4]But there will be no poor among you (for the LORD will bless you in the land which the LORD your God gives you for an inheritance to possess), [5]if only you will obey the voice of the LORD your God, being careful to do all this commandment which I command you this day. [6]For the LORD your God will bless you, as he promised you, and you shall lend to many nations, but you shall not borrow; and you shall rule over many nations, but they shall not rule over you.

7 "If there is among you a poor man, one of your brethren, in any of your towns within your land which the LORD your God gives you, you shall not harden your heart or shut your hand against your poor brother, [8]but you shall open your hand to him, and lend him sufficient for his need, whatever it may be. [9]Take heed lest there be a base thought in your heart, and you say, 'The seventh year, the year of release is near,' and your eye be hostile to your

---

14:21: Lev 11:39, 40; 17:15; Ex 23:19; 34:26. **14:22–29**: Lev 27:30–33; Num 18:21–32.

14:9 fins and scales: Scaled fish are clean, but shellfish, eels, squid, etc., are unclean.

14:11 clean birds: Most are birds that do not feed on carrion as scavengers.

14:19–20 Laws that assume knowledge of Lev 11:20–23, legislation that distinguishes between winged insects based on leg locomotion, i.e., whether they leap (clean) or crawl (unclean).

14:21 boil a kid: Presumably a cultic rite among the Canaanites. See note on Ex 23:19.

14:22–29 The law of tithing. It requires Israelite farmers to dedicate 10 percent of their annual harvest to the Lord. Part of the offering is eaten by the farmer and his family at the sanctuary (14:23), but most of it goes to the Levites (Num 18:21–23), who in turn give a tithe of what they receive to the priests (Num 18:25–32). Because the transportation of produce is difficult over long distances, provision is made to buy food offerings at the city hosting the sanctuary (14:24–26). Every third year, the tithe is stored in local facilities as provisions for the clergy and the needy (14:28–29).

15:1 seven years: A new law is added to the Sabbatical year of Ex 23:10–11 and Lev 25:1–7. In addition to letting fields lie fallow, Deuteronomy requires the remission of debts every seventh year (15:2). Periodic debt relief was designed to balance the distribution of wealth in Israel and halt the downward spiral of poverty. One problem is that creditors might be reluctant to grant loans near the end of the seven-year cycle, a point addressed by the appeal in 15:7–11.

15:3 a foreigner: Does not qualify for the sabbatical release. Deuteronomy thus erects a double standard for Israel and the people of other nations. Unlike loans made to Israelites, which are interest-free and cancelled every seventh year, loans to Gentiles are collected with interest and not subject to sabbatical cancellation (23:19–20).

15:6 over many nations: Fidelity to the covenant will raise Israel to a position of international prominence (28:1). This will be achieved briefly in the glory days of David and Solomon (2 Sam 8:1–14; 1 Kings 4:21).

15:9 cry: I.e., for divine justice on the oppressor (24:15).

poor brother, and you give him nothing, and he cry to the LORD against you, and it be sin in you. [10]You shall give to him freely, and your heart shall not be grudging when you give to him; because for this the LORD your God will bless you in all your work and in all that you undertake. [11]For the poor will never cease out of the land; therefore I command you, You shall open wide your hand to your brother, to the needy and to the poor, in the land.

12 "If your brother, a Hebrew man, or a Hebrew woman, is sold to you, he shall serve you six years, and in the seventh year you shall let him go free from you. [13]And when you let him go free from you, you shall not let him go empty-handed; [14]you shall furnish him liberally out of your flock, out of your threshing floor, and out of your wine press; as the LORD your God has blessed you, you shall give to him. [15]You shall remember that you were a slave in the land of Egypt, and the LORD your God redeemed you; therefore I command you this today. [16]But if he says to you, 'I will not go out from you,' because he loves you and your household, since he fares well with you, [17]then you shall take an awl, and thrust it through his ear into the door, and he shall be your bondman for ever. And to your bondwoman you shall do likewise. [18]It shall not seem hard to you, when you let him go free from you; for at half the cost of a hired servant he has served you six years. So the LORD your God will bless you in all that you do.

Regulations concerning Livestock

19 "All the firstling males that are born of your herd and flock you shall consecrate to the LORD your God; you shall do no work with the firstling of your herd, nor shear the firstling of your flock. [20]You shall eat it, you and your household, before the LORD your God year by year at the place which the LORD will choose. [21]But if it has any blemish, if it is lame or blind, or has any serious blemish whatever, you shall not sacrifice it to the LORD your God. [22]You shall eat it within your towns; the unclean and the clean alike may eat it, as though it were a gazelle or a deer. [23]Only you shall not eat its blood; you shall pour it out on the ground like water.

Keeping the Passover

16 "Observe the month of A'bib, and keep the Passover to the LORD your God; for in the month of Abib the LORD your God brought you out of Egypt by night. [2]And you shall offer the Passover sacrifice to the LORD your God, from the flock or the herd, at the place which the LORD will choose, to make his name dwell there. [3]You shall eat no leavened bread with it; seven days you shall eat it with unleavened bread, the bread of affliction— for you came out of the land of Egypt in hurried flight—that all the days of your life you may remember the day when you came out of the land of Egypt. [4]No leaven shall be seen with you in all your territory for seven days; nor shall any of the flesh which you sacrifice on the evening of the first day remain all night until morning. [5]You may not offer the Passover sacrifice within any of your towns which the LORD your God gives you; [6]but at the place which the LORD your God will choose, to make his name dwell in it, there you shall offer the Passover sacrifice, in the evening at the going down of the sun, at the time you came out of Egypt. [7]And you shall boil it and eat it at the place which the LORD your God will choose; and in the morning you shall turn and go to your tents. [8]For six days you shall eat unleavened bread; and on the seventh day there shall be a solemn assembly to the LORD your God; you shall do no work on it.

15:12-18: Ex 21:2–11; Lev 25:39–46.   **15:19-23:** Ex 13:11, 12; 22:30; 34:19; Num 18:17, 18.
16:1-17: Ex 23:14–17; Lev 23; Num 28–29.

15:11 the poor will never cease: The economic ideal of 15:4 will not materialize because the condition of covenant obedience in 15:5 will not be satisfied. • Jesus made the same realistic assessment in Mt 26:11 (CCC 2449).

15:12-18 The law of slave release. It upgrades the law of Ex 21:1–11 by **(1)** applying the same standard to male and female slaves and **(2)** adding that a liberated slave must be supplied with food and farm animals upon release. Without provisions, a newly released slave could easily fall back into hardship and enslavement.

15:15 you were a slave: The sabbatical release of slaves is a way of replicating Israel's Exodus from Egypt in the lives of individuals.

15:16 he loves you: Indicates that domestic slavery, though far from ideal, was not an abusive situation in ancient Israel. **he fares well:** In harsh economic conditions, slavery was actually a support system that helped to keep people without homes or farmland alive.

15:19 firstling males: Consecrated to the Lord on Passover night (Ex 13:2) as animals to be set apart for sacrifice (Ex 13:15). Blemished firstlings are ineligible for sacrifice; these

may be killed and eaten like game animals (15:21–22). For the kinds of blemishes that make animals unfit for sacrifice, see Lev 22:17–25.

16:1-17 Deuteronomy turns Israel's three major feasts into pilgrimage feasts. These are times of national assembly and worship to be celebrated, not in cities and villages throughout the land of Canaan, but at the central sanctuary (the chosen "place", 16:5-6, 11, 15). These laws expand on Ex 23:14–17, while they assume knowledge of the laws in Lev 23:1–44 and Num 28–29. See note on 12:5 and chart: *The Seven Feasts of Israel* at Lev 23.

16:1 Abib: The first month of Israel's liturgical year, later called Nisan (Esther 3:7). It falls in the spring around March-April. **Passover:** A feast commemorating Israel's Exodus from Egypt and celebrated after sundown during the first hours of Abib 15. See note on Ex 12:1–28.

16:3 the bread of affliction: Unleavened bread is a reminder of Israel's hurried escape from the afflictions of slavery in Egypt (Ex 12:33–34).

16:7 your tents: The temporary dwellings of the pilgrims who traveled to the sanctuary for the weeklong festival.

Keeping the Feast of Weeks

9 "You shall count seven weeks; begin to count the seven weeks from the time you first put the sickle to the standing grain. ¹⁰Then you shall keep the feast of weeks to the Lord your God with the tribute of a freewill offering from your hand, which you shall give as the Lord your God blesses you; ¹¹and you shall rejoice before the Lord your God, you and your son and your daughter, your manservant and your maidservant, the Levite who is within your towns, the sojourner, the fatherless, and the widow who are among you, at the place which the Lord your God will choose, to make his name dwell there. ¹²You shall remember that you were a slave in Egypt; and you shall be careful to observe these statutes.

Keeping the Feast of Booths

13 "You shall keep the feast of booths seven days, when you make your ingathering from your threshing floor and your wine press; ¹⁴you shall rejoice in your feast, you and your son and your daughter, your manservant and your maidservant, the Levite, the sojourner, the fatherless, and the widow who are within your towns. ¹⁵For seven days you shall keep the feast to the Lord your God at the place which the Lord will choose; because the Lord your God will bless you in all your produce and in all the work of your hands, so that you will be altogether joyful.

16 "Three times a year all your males shall appear before the Lord your God at the place which he will choose: at the feast of unleavened bread, at the feast of weeks, and at the feast of booths. They shall not appear before the Lord empty-handed; ¹⁷every man shall give as he is able, according to the blessing of the Lord your God which he has given you.

Appointing Judges and Officers

18 "You shall appoint judges and officers in all your towns which the Lord your God gives you,

according to your tribes; and they shall judge the people with righteous judgment. ¹⁹You shall not pervert justice; you shall not show partiality; and you shall not take a bribe, for a bribe blinds the eyes of the wise and subverts the cause of the righteous. ²⁰Justice, and only justice, you shall follow, that you may live and inherit the land which the Lord your God gives you.

Forbidden Forms of Worship

21 "You shall not plant any tree as an Ashe'rah beside the altar of the Lord your God which you shall make. ²²And you shall not set up a pillar, which the Lord your God hates.

17 "You shall not sacrifice to the Lord your God an ox or a sheep in which is a blemish, any defect whatever; for that is an abomination to the Lord your God.

2 "If there is found among you, within any of your towns which the Lord your God gives you, a man or woman who does what is evil in the sight of the Lord your God, in transgressing his covenant, ³and has gone and served other gods and worshiped them, or the sun or the moon or any of the host of heaven, which I have forbidden, ⁴and it is told you and you hear of it; then you shall inquire diligently, and if it is true and certain that such an abominable thing has been done in Israel, ⁵then you shall bring forth to your gates that man or woman who has done this evil thing, and you shall stone that man or woman to death with stones. ⁶On the evidence of two witnesses or of three witnesses he that is to die shall be put to death; a person shall not be put to death on the evidence of one witness. ⁷The hand of the witnesses shall be first against him to put him to death, and afterward the hand of all the people. So you shall purge the evil from the midst of you.

Legal Decisions by Priests and Judges

8 "If any case arises requiring decision between one kind of homicide and another, one kind of

---

16:19: Ex 23:6–9; Lev 19:15. **16:21, 22**: Lev 26:1. **17:1**: Lev 22:17–24. **17:2–7**: Ex 22:20. **17:6**: Num 35:30; Deut 19:15; Mt 18:16; 2 Cor 13:1; 1 Tim 5:19; Heb 10:28. **17:7**: Deut 19:19; 1 Cor 5:13.

16:9 first put the sickle: An armful of barley stalks was cut from the field during Passover week. See note on Lev 23:11.

16:10 feast of weeks: Celebrated in late spring, also called the feast of "harvest" (Ex 23:16) or "Pentecost" (Tob 2:1).

16:13 feast of booths: Celebrated in autumn, also called the feast of "ingathering" (Ex 23:16) or "Tabernacles" (Jn 7:2). Every seventh year, the laws of Deuteronomy were read aloud to the pilgrims assembled for this feast (31:10–13).

16:18 judges and officers: Arbiters of civil disputes (25:1). Deuteronomy does not specify who manned these local tribunals, but it seems likely that both Levites and laymen were represented (19:17; 21:19; 22:15). Recall that the priestly tribe of Levi settled in various cities throughout the tribal territories in Israel (Josh 21:8–42).

16:21 Asherah: The name of a Canaanite fertility goddess. Asherah worship ensnared Israel at various times in its history (Judg 3:7; 2 Kings 17:10).

16:22 pillar: A cultic stone monument.

17:1 blemish: Any physical deformity or irregularity (Lev 22:17–25).

17:2–7 Idolatry is a crime in Israelite law (as in 13:1–18).

17:3 served other gods: Idolatry is a betrayal of the Lord, who demands exclusive allegiance from his people (5:6–7; 6:14–15). **the sun or the moon:** Objects of worship in the ancient Near East (4:19).

17:6 two witnesses: Allegations had to be verified by multiple witnesses for a death sentence to be issued in Israel. As further legal protection for the accused, the Law threatens false witnesses with capital punishment as well (19:15–19).

17:8–13 A federal court is established to handle difficult cases passed up from the local courts. Members of this supreme tribunal convene in the "place" chosen by God (17:8, eventually the city of Jerusalem). Failure to comply with its decisions is an offense worthy of death (17:12).

legal right and another, or one kind of assault and another, any case within your towns which is too difficult for you, then you shall arise and go up to the place which the LORD your God will choose, ⁹and coming to the Levitical priests, and to the judge who is in office in those days, you shall consult them, and they shall declare to you the decision. ¹⁰Then you shall do according to what they declare to you from that place which the LORD will choose; and you shall be careful to do according to all that they direct you; ¹¹according to the instructions which they give you, and according to the decision which they pronounce to you, you shall do; you shall not turn aside from the verdict which they declare to you, either to the right hand or to the left. ¹²The man who acts presumptuously, by not obeying the priest who stands to minister there before the LORD your God, or the judge, that man shall die; so you shall purge the evil from Israel. ¹³And all the people shall hear, and fear, and not act presumptuously again.

Limitations of Royal Authority

14 "When you come to the land which the LORD your God gives you, and you possess it and dwell in it, and then say, 'I will set a king over me, like all the nations that are round about me'; ¹⁵you may indeed set as king over you him whom the LORD your God will choose. One from among your brethren you shall set as king over you; you may not put a foreigner over you, who is not your brother. ¹⁶Only he must not multiply horses for himself, or cause the people to return to Egypt in order to multiply horses, since the LORD has said to you, 'You shall never return that way again.' ¹⁷And he shall not multiply wives for himself, lest his heart turn away; nor shall he greatly multiply for himself silver and gold.

18 "And when he sits on the throne of his kingdom, he shall write for himself in a book a copy of this law, from that which is in the charge of the Levitical priests; ¹⁹and it shall be with him, and he shall read in it all the days of his life, that he may learn to fear the LORD his God, by keeping all the words of this law and these statutes, and doing them; ²⁰that his heart may not be lifted up above his brethren, and that he may not turn aside from the commandment, either to the right hand or to the left; so that he may continue long in his kingdom, he and his children, in Israel.

Privileges of Priests and Levites

18 "The Levitical priests, that is, all the tribe of Levi, shall have no portion or inheritance with Israel; they shall eat the offerings by fire to the LORD, and his rightful dues. ²They shall have no inheritance among their brethren; the LORD is their inheritance, as he promised them. ³And this shall be the priests' due from the people, from those offering a sacrifice, whether it be ox or sheep: they shall give to the priest the shoulder and the two cheeks and the stomach. ⁴The first fruits of your grain, of your wine and of your oil, and the first of the fleece of your sheep, you shall give him. ⁵For the LORD your God has chosen him out of all your tribes, to stand and minister in the name of the LORD, him and his sons for ever.

6 "And if a Levite comes from any of your towns out of all Israel, where he lives—and he may come when he desires—to the place which the LORD will choose, ⁷then he may minister in the name of the LORD his God, like all his fellow Levites who stand to minister there before the LORD. ⁸They shall have equal portions to eat, besides what he receives from the sale of his patrimony.ᵐ

18:1–8: Num 18:20–24.

17:12 the priest: The high priest in particular (2 Chron 19:11). **the judge:** Eventually the king of Israel (2 Sam 14:3–20) or someone appointed by him (2 Chron 19:8–11).

17:14–20 The law of the king, which goes into effect when Israel founds a monarchy (fulfilled in 1 Sam 8:4–22). The elevation of a human king will be a divine concession to the weakness of Israel, who will become dissatisfied with the Lord's kingship over his people (33:5; 1 Sam 8:7). Among the dangers in adopting this model of government, Deuteronomy foresees that a future king will be tempted to amass weapons, wives, and wealth for himself, thus placing a significant burden upon the people. It is precisely these types of selfish excess that will trigger the downfall of Israelite kings such as Solomon (1 Kings 10:26—11:8).

17:14 like all the nations: Kingship was a near-universal institution in the ancient Near East.

17:15 among your brethren: The king must be a fellow Israelite.

17:16 horses: Used for mounted archers and battle chariots. The king is warned not to import warhorses from Egypt,

lest he seek security in a strong military rather than in the Lord (20:1).

17:18 a copy of this law: A personal copy of Deuteronomy. The official scroll was entrusted to the Levitical priests (31:9) and kept in the sanctuary beside the Ark of the Covenant (31:24–26). The king must be an exemplary student of the Torah if his rule is to please the Lord and his royal family is to enjoy a long reign.

18:1 The Levitical priests: A general term for Israel's ministers of worship. Legislation found in Exodus, Leviticus, and Numbers makes a clear distinction between "priests" (those who offer sacrifice and incense) and "Levites" (assistants to the priests and movers of the sanctuary), but Deuteronomy is not concerned with this difference, probably because it focuses on civil rather than ceremonial law. **the tribe of Levi:** Descendants of the patriarch Levi, the son of Jacob (Ex 6:16–25). Its priests stand in the family line of Aaron and his sons (Ex 40:12–15). **no portion:** Levi is the one landless tribe in Israel. Unlike the lay tribes, who will each inherit territories in Canaan, the Levites will disperse throughout the land to live in 48 cities (Josh 21:8–42).

18:3 shoulder … stomach: Food portions reserved for the ministering priest (cf. Num 18:8–32).

18:8 patrimony: Family homes and possessions sold for money (Lev 25:32).

ᵐHeb obscure.

Abominable Practices Prohibited

9 "When you come into the land which the Lord your God gives you, you shall not learn to follow the abominable practices of those nations. [10]There shall not be found among you any one who burns his son or his daughter as an offering,[n] any one who practices divination, a soothsayer, or an augur, or a sorcerer, [11]or a charmer, or a medium, or a wizard, or a necromancer. [12]For whoever does these things is an abomination to the Lord; and because of these abominable practices the Lord your God is driving them out before you. [13]You shall be blameless before the Lord your God. [14]For these nations, which you are about to dispossess, give heed to soothsayers and to diviners; but as for you, the Lord your God has not allowed you so to do.

15 "The Lord your God will raise up for you a prophet like me from among you, from your brethren—him you shall heed—[16]just as you desired of the Lord your God at Horeb on the day of the assembly, when you said, 'Let me not hear again the voice of the Lord my God, or see this great fire any more, lest I die.' [17]And the Lord said to me, 'They have rightly said all that they have spoken. [18]I will raise up for them a prophet* like you from among their brethren; and I will put my words in his mouth, and he shall speak to them all that I command him. [19]And whoever will not give heed to my words which he shall speak in my name, I myself will require it of him. [20]But the prophet who presumes to speak a word in my name which I have not commanded him to speak, or who speaks in the name of other gods, that same prophet shall die.' [21]And if you say in your heart, 'How may we know the word which the Lord has not spoken?'—[22]when a prophet speaks in the name of the Lord, if the word does not come to pass or come true, that is a word which the Lord has not spoken; the prophet has spoken it presumptuously, you need not be afraid of him.

Cities of Refuge

19 "When the Lord your God cuts off the nations whose land the Lord your God gives you, and you dispossess them and dwell in their cities and in their houses, [2]you shall set apart three cities for you in the land which the Lord your God gives you to possess. [3]You shall prepare the roads, and divide into three parts the area of the land which the Lord your God gives you as a possession, so that any manslayer can flee to them.

4 "This is the provision for the manslayer, who by fleeing there may save his life. If any one kills his neighbor unintentionally without having been at enmity with him in time past—[5]as when a man goes into the forest with his neighbor to cut wood, and his hand swings the axe to cut down a tree, and the head slips from the handle and strikes his neighbor so that he dies—he may flee to one of these cities and save his life; [6]lest the avenger of blood in hot anger pursue the manslayer and overtake him, because the way is long, and wound him mortally, though the man did not deserve to die, since he was not at enmity with his neighbor in time past. [7]Therefore I command you, You shall set apart three

---

18:10, 11: Ex 22:18; Lev 19:26, 31; 20:6, 27.   18:13: Mt 5:48.   18:15–19: Acts 3:22, 23; 7:37.   19:1–13: Ex 21:12–14; Num 35.

18:9–14 Deuteronomy condemns pagan superstition and witchcraft. In the ancient Near East, occult practitioners often sought to learn about or influence events of the future. To this end, they engaged in such things as fortune-telling (diviners, soothsayers, augurs), black magic (sorcerers, charmers), and communication with the dead (mediums, wizards, necromancers). It is significant that these laws immediately precede Moses' instruction regarding true prophecy in Israel (18:15–22). The implied message: God reveals his will and his plans to his prophets, not to pagan spiritists (CCC 2116–117).

18:10 burns his son: Child sacrifice was part of the Canaanite cult of Molech (Lev 18:21).

18:15 a prophet like me: One who will speak the word of the Lord to his people. Moses himself is the model who defines the expectation, suggesting the prophet to come will be a ruler, preacher, lawgiver, intercessor, wonderworker, and foreseer of the future (31:29; 34:10). Many scholars think the passage envisions the rise of prophetic ministry in Israel and not simply the coming of a special individual. • That said, Jewish expectations during NT times identified the prophet like Moses with Israel's Messiah. This can be seen in the Dead Sea Scrolls as well as the Gospel of John ("the prophet", Jn

1:21; 6:14; 7:40). Regardless, then, of how this prediction might apply to various prophets in the OT, the expectation of a prophet like Moses is ultimately fulfilled in Jesus Christ (Acts 3:22; 7:37). This is first revealed at the Transfiguration of Jesus, in which the words "listen to him" (Mt 17:5; Mk 9:7) harken back to the announcement, **him you shall heed** (see Greek LXX).

18:22 does not come to pass: A prophet is proven false when his predictions fail to come true. He is also exposed as a fraud if he speaks in the name of other gods (18:20) or urges people to worship gods other than the Lord (13:1–3).

19:1–13 Deuteronomy distinguishes between manslaughter (19:1–10) and murder (19:11–13). Manslaughter is accidental and is not punishable by death, whereas murder requires intent and premeditation, for which culprits are subject to the death penalty.

19:2 three cities: Cities of refuge for manslayers. Three asylum cities had already been assigned east of the Jordan (4:41–43); now three more are assigned west of the Jordan. Deuteronomy builds on Num 35:9–34, adding **(1)** that roads must be constructed for easy access to these sites (19:3) and **(2)** that additional cities may be designated for asylum if Israel's territory expands to the full extent that God desires (19:8–9). The cities of refuge are listed by name and location in Josh 20:1–9.

19:6 avenger of blood: A kinsman of the victim who, in tribal societies, tracks down and takes the life of the manslayer. See word study: *Redeem* at Lev 25:25.

---

*18:18: The prophet like Moses mentioned here refers either to the prophetic movement as a whole or to an individual, either Joshua (successor of Moses) or Samuel. The New Testament sees here a reference to the Messiah; cf. Jn 1:21; Acts 3:22; 7:37.

[n] Heb *makes his son or his daughter pass through the fire.*

cities. [8]And if the LORD your God enlarges your border, as he has sworn to your fathers, and gives you all the land which he promised to give to your fathers—[9]provided you are careful to keep all this commandment, which I command you this day, by loving the LORD your God and by walking ever in his ways—then you shall add three other cities to these three, [10]lest innocent blood be shed in your land which the LORD your God gives you for an inheritance, and so the guilt of bloodshed be upon you.

11 "But if any man hates his neighbor, and lies in wait for him, and attacks him, and wounds him mortally so that he dies, and the man flees into one of these cities, [12]then the elders of his city shall send and fetch him from there, and hand him over to the avenger of blood, so that he may die. [13]Your eye shall not pity him, but you shall purge the guilt of innocent blood° from Israel, so that it may be well with you.

Concerning Landmarks

14 "In the inheritance which you will hold in the land that the LORD your God gives you to possess, you shall not remove your neighbor's landmark, which the men of old have set.

Concerning Witnesses

15 "A single witness shall not prevail against a man for any crime or for any wrong in connection with any offense that he has committed; only on the evidence of two witnesses, or of three witnesses, shall a charge be sustained. [16]If a malicious witness rises against any man to accuse him of wrongdoing, [17]then both parties to the dispute shall appear before the LORD, before the priests and the judges who are in office in those days; [18]the judges shall inquire diligently, and if the witness is a false witness and has accused his brother falsely, [19]then you shall do to him as he had meant to do to his brother; so you shall purge the evil from the midst of you. [20]And the rest shall hear, and fear, and shall never again commit any such evil among you. [21]Your eye shall not pity; it shall be life for life, eye for eye, tooth for tooth, hand for hand, foot for foot.

Concerning Warfare

20 "When you go forth to war against your enemies, and see horses and chariots and an army larger than your own, you shall not be afraid of them; for the LORD your God is with you, who brought you up out of the land of Egypt. [2]And when you draw near to the battle, the priest shall come forward and speak to the people, [3]and shall say to them, 'Hear, O Israel, you draw near this day to battle against your enemies: let not your heart faint; do not fear, or tremble, or be in dread of them; [4]for the LORD your God is he that goes with you, to fight for you against your enemies, to give you the victory.' [5]Then the officers shall speak to the people, saying, 'What man is there that has built a new house and has not dedicated it? Let him go back to his house, lest he die in the battle and another man dedicate it. [6]And what man is there that has planted a vineyard and has not enjoyed its fruit? Let him go back to his house, lest he die in the battle and another man enjoy its fruit. [7]And what man is there that has betrothed a wife and has not taken her? Let him go back to his house, lest he die in the battle and another man take her.' [8]And the officers shall speak further to the people, and say, 'What man is there that is fearful and fainthearted? Let him go back to his house, lest the heart of his fellows melt as his heart.' [9]And when the officers have made an end of speaking to the people, then commanders shall be appointed at the head of the people.

10 "When you draw near to a city to fight against it, offer terms of peace to it. [11]And if its answer to

---

19:15: Num 35:30; Deut 17:6; Mt 18:16; 2 Cor 13:1; 1 Tim 5:19; Heb 10:28.   **19:16–20:** Ex 20:16; 23:1; Lev 19:16; Deut 5:20.   **19:19:** 1 Cor 5:13.   **19:21:** Ex 21:23–26; Lev 24:20; Mt 5:38.

19:8 enlarges your border: To the full dimensions specified in 1:7–8.

19:14 landmark: Probably stones used as boundary markers. Moving them is illegal, since it would lead to encroachment and property disputes.

19:15–21 The law of witnesses, stipulating that no crime can be prosecuted in Israel unless two or more eyewitnesses can corroborate an allegation of wrongdoing. Legal protection is afforded the innocent by making false testimony a crime in its own right. Note that perjurers receive the same punishment they intended for the one falsely accused (19:19).

19:17 priests . . . judges: The local judicial council (16:18).

19:21 eye for eye: A standard of strict proportion between crimes and their punishment. Justice is compromised if the penalty either exceeds or falls short of the severity of the offense. See note on Ex 21:24.

20:1–20 Deuteronomy's warfare laws, which give instruction on spiritual leadership in times of conflict (20:2–4), on combat exemptions (20:5–9), and on rules of engagement for the siege of a walled city (20:10–20).

20:2 the priest: Most likely the high priest, whose task is to rouse the faith of the troops, so that Israel relies, not on its own strength, but on the mighty power of God. Trust in the Lord will be needed when the people enter Canaan and face larger and better-equipped armies (e.g., Josh 11:1–9).

20:5–9 To be exempt from combat duty, a soldier must have **(1)** built a new house, **(2)** planted a new vineyard, **(3)** betrothed a new wife, or **(4)** lost all courage to fight (1 Mac 3:56).

20:10–18 The rules of siege warfare, which differ according to the location of the city under attack. **(1)** *Subjugation* is the normal means of dealing with cities outside the land of Canaan; however, if surrender is refused, the city's defenders are marked for death and wide allowance is given to plunder the city of spoils (20:10–15). **(2)** *Extermination* is mandated for cities inside the land of Canaan, meaning their inhabitants are placed under a ban of total destruction that leaves no survivors (20:16–18). For reasons behind this extreme policy in dealing with the Canaanites, see essay: *The Conquest of Canaan* at Josh 6.

°Or *the blood of the innocent.*

you is peace and it opens to you, then all the people who are found in it shall do forced labor for you and shall serve you. ¹²But if it makes no peace with you, but makes war against you, then you shall besiege it; ¹³and when the Lᴏʀᴅ your God gives it into your hand you shall put all its males to the sword, ¹⁴but the women and the little ones, the cattle, and everything else in the city, all its spoil, you shall take as booty for yourselves; and you shall enjoy the spoil of your enemies, which the Lᴏʀᴅ your God has given you. ¹⁵Thus you shall do to all the cities which are very far from you, which are not cities of the nations here. ¹⁶But in the cities of these peoples that the Lᴏʀᴅ your God gives you for an inheritance, you shall save alive nothing that breathes, ¹⁷but you shall utterly destroy them, the Hittites and the Am′orites, the Canaanites and the Per′izzites, the Hi′vites and the Jeb′usites, as the Lᴏʀᴅ your God has commanded; ¹⁸that they may not teach you to do according to all their abominable practices which they have done in the service of their gods, and so to sin against the Lᴏʀᴅ your God.

19 "When you besiege a city for a long time, making war against it in order to take it, you shall not destroy its trees by wielding an axe against them; for you may eat of them, but you shall not cut them down. Are the trees in the field men that they should be besieged by you? ²⁰Only the trees which you know are not trees for food you may destroy and cut down that you may build siege-works against the city that makes war with you, until it falls.

Concerning the Slain

21 "If in the land which the Lᴏʀᴅ your God gives you to possess, any one is found slain, lying in the open country, and it is not known who killed him, ²then your elders and your judges shall come forth, and they shall measure the distance

to the cities which are around him that is slain; ³and the elders of the city which is nearest to the slain man shall take a heifer which has never been worked and which has not pulled in the yoke. ⁴And the elders of that city shall bring the heifer down to a valley with running water, which is neither plowed nor sown, and shall break the heifer's neck there in the valley. ⁵And the priests the sons of Levi shall come forward, for the Lᴏʀᴅ your God has chosen them to minister to him and to bless in the name of the Lᴏʀᴅ, and by their word every dispute and every assault shall be settled. ⁶And all the elders of that city nearest to the slain man shall wash their hands over the heifer whose neck was broken in the valley; ⁷and they shall testify, 'Our hands did not shed this blood, neither did our eyes see it shed. ⁸Forgive, O Lᴏʀᴅ, your people Israel, whom you have redeemed, and set not the guilt of innocent blood in the midst of your people Israel; but let the guilt of blood be forgiven them.' ⁹So you shall purge the guilt of innocent blood from your midst, when you do what is right in the sight of the Lᴏʀᴅ.

Women Taken Captive

10 "When you go forth to war against your enemies, and the Lᴏʀᴅ your God gives them into your hands, and you take them captive, ¹¹and see among the captives a beautiful woman, and you have desire for her and would take her for yourself as wife, ¹²then you shall bring her home to your house, and she shall shave her head and pare her nails. ¹³And she shall put off her captive's garb, and shall remain in your house and bewail her father and her mother a full month; after that you may go in to her, and be her husband, and she shall be your wife. ¹⁴Then, if you have no delight in her, you shall let her go where she will; but you shall not sell her for money, you shall not treat her as a slave, since you have humiliated her.

20:17 utterly destroy: The ban of total destruction, which is a means of dedicating a city to the Lord. See word study: *Devoted* at Josh 6:17. **Hittites ... Jebusites:** Pagan peoples who occupied Canaan before Israel's invasion of the land (7:1). According to a Jewish tradition in the *Book of Jubilees*, which dates to the second century B.C., the world was divided into territories after the flood and assigned to the sons of Noah; each son swore an oath to settle his allotted portion and not encroach upon lands belonging to others. Palestine was given to Shem and his descendants (the Israelites), but in time Ham and his descendants (the Canaanites) seized it for themselves. Against this background, Israel's conquest of Canaan was **(1)** an effort to reclaim territory that rightfully belonged to the Shemites and **(2)** an administration of the curse that the Hamites brought upon themselves when they violated their oath.

20:19 trees: Israel is forbidden to axe down fruit and olive trees in order to build the wooden implements of siege warfare. Deforesting the woodlands around a city is a practice known from Near Eastern war annals.

21:1–9 The law for unsolved homicides. If the body of a murder victim is found and the culprit remains unknown, the town nearest the crime scene must conduct an atonement ritual to purge the land of bloodguilt. Sin, it is implied, is not a private matter with only private consequences but is something that endangers the whole covenant people (21:8). That bloodshed defiles the land, see Num 35:31–34.

21:4 break the heifer's neck: Some take this to mean "cut the heifer's throat".

21:11 beautiful woman: One who is taken captive in a military expedition outside the land of Canaan (20:14–15).

21:12 shave ... pare: Symbolic of cutting away her past life in preparation for a new life in Israel. • *Morally,* as an Israelite was allowed to marry a captive woman after shaving her head and trimming her nails, so we are permitted to embrace what is useful in secular wisdom, so long as we cut away what is offensive to Christian truth (St. Jerome, *Letters* 21, 13).

21:14 let her go: The law protects an unwanted wife from being treated like property to be sold for gain.

Right of the First-born Son

15 "If a man has two wives, the one loved and the other disliked, and they have borne him children, both the loved and the disliked, and if the first-born son is hers that is disliked, [16]then on the day when he assigns his possessions as an inheritance to his sons, he may not treat the son of the loved as the first-born in preference to the son of the disliked, who is the first-born, [17]but he shall acknowledge the first-born, the son of the disliked, by giving him a double portion of all that he has, for he is the first issue of his strength; the right of the first-born is his.

Rebellious Sons

18 "If a man has a stubborn and rebellious son, who will not obey the voice of his father or the voice of his mother, and, though they chastise him, will not give heed to them, [19]then his father and his mother shall take hold of him and bring him out to the elders of his city at the gate of the place where he lives, [20]and they shall say to the elders of his city, 'This our son is stubborn and rebellious, he will not obey our voice; he is a glutton and a drunkard.' [21]Then all the men of the city shall stone him to death with stones; so you shall purge the evil from your midst; and all Israel shall hear, and fear.

Miscellaneous Laws

22 "And if a man has committed a crime punishable by death and he is put to death, and you hang him on a tree, [23]his body shall not remain all night upon the tree, but you shall bury him the same day, for a hanged man is accursed by God; you shall not defile your land which the LORD your God gives you for an inheritance.

22 "You shall not see your brother's ox or his sheep go astray, and withhold your help[p] from them; you shall take them back to your brother. [2]And if he is not near you, or if you do not know him, you shall bring it home to your house, and it shall be with you until your brother seeks it; then you shall restore it to him. [3]And so you shall do with his donkey; so you shall do with his garment; so you shall do with any lost thing of your brother's, which he loses and you find; you may not withhold your help. [4]You shall not see your brother's donkey or his ox fallen down by the way, and withhold your help[p] from them; you shall help him to lift them up again.

5 "A woman shall not wear anything that pertains to a man, nor shall a man put on a woman's garment; for whoever does these things is an abomination to the LORD your God.

6 "If you chance to come upon a bird's nest, in any tree or on the ground, with young ones or eggs and the mother sitting upon the young or upon the eggs, you shall not take the mother with the young; [7]you shall let the mother go, but the young you may

---

21:18–21: Ex 20:12; 21:15, 17; Lev 20:9; Deut 5:16; 27:16.   **21:22:** Acts 5:30; 10:39.
21:23: Gal 3:13.   **22:1–4:** Ex 23:4, 5.

21:15–17 The law of primogeniture, which protects the inheritance of a first-born son. Without this legal safeguard, a father could bequeath a double portion of his estate to a younger son as a sign of his preferential love for the younger son's mother. Note that Deuteronomy does not create the right of the first-born son; rather, it guards against the abuse of a custom that is already ancient (Gen 25:24–34). • The law of primogeniture recalls various family struggles in the Book of Genesis, e.g., the story of Abraham giving the first-born inheritance to Isaac (son of Sarah), even though Ishmael was his oldest (son of Hagar), and the story of Jacob bestowing a first-born blessing to Joseph (son of Rachael), even though Reuben was his oldest (son of Leah).

21:15 two wives: Deuteronomy tolerates bigamy, although marriage to more than one wife at a time deviates from the standard of monogamy instituted at creation (Gen 2:24).

21:17 double portion: Either "twice" the inheritance received by the younger sons or possibly "two-thirds" of the father's total possessions (the same Hebrew term appears in Zech 13:8).

21:18 rebellious son: A wild and defiant young man. Rebellion in this context is not occasional misbehavior but a life-style of wantonness. The son has dishonored his parents by disregarding their instruction (**voice**) and discipline (**chastise**). The law assumes that mother and father are both expected to play a part in the moral upbringing of their children.

21:19 the gate: The place in a walled city where elders assembled as tribunals to make civil and judicial rulings (22:15; 25:7).

21:20 a glutton and a drunkard: Excessive consumption of food and alcohol points to a self-indulgent life-style (Prov 23:20). • Jesus was wrongly accused of gluttony and drunkenness because of his table fellowship with tax collectors and sinners (Mt 11:19).

21:22 hang him on a tree: Not the manner of execution but a public display of the criminal's corpse after execution. This gruesome spectacle, with the body tied or impaled to a tree or wooden upright, stood as a warning against lawless behavior in Israel. A similar ritual was conducted to ridicule conquered enemies in war (Josh 8:29; 10:26). Deuteronomy regulates the practice by mandating the burial of the felon before sundown (21:23).

21:23 accursed: The curse is manifest in the execution of the felon and the exhibition of his body. Other passages imply the criminal must bear the curse of shame and death for his own wrongdoing, lest the wrath of God flame out against all Israel (Num 25:4; 2 Sam 21:1–9). Later Jewish texts relate this punishment to crucifixion (e.g., Dead Sea Scrolls, 11QT 64). • Paul also cites this passage in connection with the Crucifixion of Jesus, whose body was hung on a tree to bear the curse of the broken Mosaic covenant (Gal 3:13).

22:1–4 Expands the law of lost property in Ex 23:4 with greater stress on neighborly love. The right to private ownership is assumed.

22:5 wear anything: Cross-dressing is forbidden. It is implied that transvestism is a rebellion against nature and thus a rebellion against the Lord, who created the sexual distinction between man and woman (Gen 1:27).

---

[p] Heb *hide yourself.*

take to yourself; that it may go well with you, and
that you may live long.
8 "When you build a new house, you shall make
a parapet for your roof, that you may not bring
the guilt of blood upon your house, if any one fall
from it.
9 "You shall not sow your vineyard with two
kinds of seed, lest the whole yield be forfeited to the
sanctuary,[q] the crop which you have sown and
the yield of the vineyard. [10]You shall not plow with
an ox and a donkey together. [11]You shall not wear a
mingled stuff, wool and linen together.
12 "You shall make yourself tassels on the four
corners of your cloak with which you cover yourself.

Concerning Sexual Relations

13 "If any man takes a wife, and goes in to
her, and then spurns her, [14]and charges her with
shameful conduct, and brings an evil name upon
her, saying, 'I took this woman, and when I came
near her, I did not find in her the tokens of virginity,'
[15]then the father of the young woman and her
mother shall take and bring out the tokens of her
virginity to the elders of the city in the gate; [16]and
the father of the young woman shall say to the
elders, 'I gave my daughter to this man to wife, and
he spurns her; [17]and behold, he has made shameful
charges against her, saying, "I did not find in your
daughter the tokens of virginity." And yet these
are the tokens of my daughter's virginity.' And
they shall spread the garment before the elders
of the city. [18]Then the elders of that city shall take
the man and whip him; [19]and they shall fine him
a hundred shekels of silver, and give them to the
father of the young woman, because he has brought
an evil name upon a virgin of Israel; and she shall
be his wife; he may not put her away all his days.
[20]But if the thing is true, that the tokens of virginity
were not found in the young woman, [21]then they
shall bring out the young woman to the door of her
father's house, and the men of her city shall stone
her to death with stones, because she has wrought
folly in Israel by playing the harlot in her father's
house; so you shall purge the evil from the midst
of you.
22 "If a man is found lying with the wife of
another man, both of them shall die, the man who
lay with the woman, and the woman; so you shall
purge the evil from Israel.
23 "If there is a betrothed virgin, and a man
meets her in the city and lies with her, [24]then you
shall bring them both out to the gate of that city,
and you shall stone them to death with stones, the
young woman because she did not cry for help
though she was in the city, and the man because he
violated his neighbor's wife; so you shall purge the
evil from the midst of you.
25 "But if in the open country a man meets a
young woman who is betrothed, and the man seizes
her and lies with her, then only the man who lay
with her shall die. [26]But to the young woman you
shall do nothing; in the young woman there is no
offense punishable by death, for this case is like that
of a man attacking and murdering his neighbor;
[27]because he came upon her in the open country, and
though the betrothed young woman cried for help
there was no one to rescue her.
28 "If a man meets a virgin who is not betrothed,
and seizes her and lies with her, and they are found,
[29]then the man who lay with her shall give to the
father of the young woman fifty shekels of silver,

22:9–11: Lev 19:19. **22:12:** Num 15:37–41. **22:21:** 1 Cor 5:13. **22:22–27:** Ex 20:14; Lev 18:20; 20:10; Deut 5:18. **22:24:** 1 Cor 5:13. **22:28, 29:** Ex 22:16, 17.

22:8 a parapet: A wall around the outer edge of a rooftop. This precaution is mandatory, since various types of work were done on the roof, and homeowners were liable for any injuries or fatalities resulting from an accidental fall.

22:9–11 Laws against mixing. They signify that Israel is a people set apart from other nations and their heathen practices. See note on Lev 19:19.

22:9 forfeited: I.e., handed over to the sanctuary as an offering.

22:10 an ox and a donkey: This would make it difficult to steer and control the plow, as the ox is stronger, but the donkey is faster. In addition, the Torah classifies an ox as a clean animal (14:4) and a donkey as an unclean animal (Lev 11:26). • Paul seems to allude to this law when he advises believers not to yoke themselves to unbelievers in ways that could endanger their faith (2 Cor 6:14).

22:12 tassels: Blue fringes that serve as reminders of the Lord's commands (Num 15:37–40).

22:14 tokens of virginity: A bloodstained sheet or piece of clothing. It was kept by the bride's parents to verify that she was a virgin on her wedding night.

22:18 whip him: In accord with the disciplinary law of 25:1–3.

22:19 fine him: As compensation for the public disgrace he brought upon the bride and her family by his unfounded accusation in 22:14. **may not put her away:** Divorce is not a legal option in this case (24:1–4).

22:22–30 Penal laws for sexual crimes such as adultery (22:22–24), rape (22:25–29), and sexual involvement with a stepmother (22:30). Consensual adultery between married persons, as well as the rape of another man's bride, warrants the death penalty (22:22, 24, 25).

22:23 betrothed: Betrothal is the initial stage of marriage in which a couple becomes husband and wife by mutual consent but do not yet consummate their marriage by sexual union. The Mosaic Law thus considers betrothed couples to be legally married.

22:24 did not cry for help: From a legal standpoint, the failure to sound a distress call implies that the woman gave free consent to have relations with the man.

22:29 may not put her away: Divorce is not a legal option in this case (24:1–4). Essentially this law protects the long-term welfare of the woman, lest, having been victimized already, she then be discarded to fend for herself.

[q]Heb *become holy.*

and she shall be his wife, because he has violated her; he may not put her away all his days.

30 r "A man shall not take his father's wife, nor shall he uncover her who is his father's. s

Exclusion from the Assembly

23 "He whose testicles are crushed or whose male member is cut off shall not enter the assembly of the Lord.

2 "No bastard shall enter the assembly of the Lord; even to the tenth generation none of his descendants shall enter the assembly of the Lord.

3 "No Am'monite or Moabite shall enter the assembly of the Lord; even to the tenth generation none belonging to them shall enter the assembly of the Lord for ever; 4because they did not meet you with bread and with water on the way, when you came forth out of Egypt, and because they hired against you Balaam the son of Beor from Pe'thor of Mesopota'mia, to curse you. 5Nevertheless the Lord your God would not listen to Balaam; but the Lord your God turned the curse into a blessing for you, because the Lord your God loved you. 6You shall not seek their peace or their prosperity all your days for ever.

7 "You shall not abhor an E'domite, for he is your brother; you shall not abhor an Egyptian, because you were a sojourner in his land. 8The children of the third generation that are born to them may enter the assembly of the Lord.

Sanitary, Ritual, and Humanitarian Precepts

9 "When you go forth against your enemies and are in camp, then you shall keep yourself from every evil thing.

10 "If there is among you any man who is not clean by reason of a nocturnal emission, then he shall go outside the camp, he shall not come within the camp; 11but when evening comes on, he shall bathe himself in water, and when the sun is down, he may come within the camp.

12 "You shall have a place outside the camp and you shall go out to it; 13and you shall have a stick with your weapons; and when you relieve yourself outside, you shall dig a hole with it, and turn back and cover up your excrement. 14Because the Lord your God walks in the midst of your camp, to save you and to give up your enemies before you, therefore your camp must be holy, that he may not see anything indecent among you, and turn away from you.

15 "You shall not give up to his master a slave who has escaped from his master to you; 16he shall dwell with you, in your midst, in the place which he shall choose within one of your towns, where it pleases him best; you shall not oppress him.

17 "There shall be no cult prostitute of the daughters of Israel, neither shall there be a cult prostitute of the sons of Israel. 18You shall not bring the hire of a harlot, or the wages of a dog, t into the house of the Lord your God in payment for any vow; for both of these are an abomination to the Lord your God.

19 "You shall not lend upon interest to your brother, interest on money, interest on victuals, interest on anything that is lent for interest. 20To a foreigner you may lend upon interest, but to your brother you shall not lend upon interest; that the Lord your God may bless you in all that you undertake in the land which you are entering to take possession of it.

21 "When you make a vow to the Lord your God, you shall not be slack to pay it; for the Lord your God will surely require it of you, and it would be sin in you. 22But if you refrain from vowing, it shall be no sin in you. 23You shall be careful to perform what

---

23:19: Ex 22:26; Lev 25:35–37.   **23:21–23**: Num 30:2–16.

22:30 father's wife: Sexual involvement with a stepmother is not only forbidden (Lev 18:8) but is punished by death (Lev 20:11) and subject to a special curse (27:20). Use of the verb "take" (as in 24:1) suggests this law prohibits marriage to a stepmother.

23:1 assembly of the Lord: Probably the community of Israel gathered for worship rather than the people of Israel more generally. Understood in this way, liturgical festivals are off-limits to eunuchs (23:1), illegitimate children (23:2), and Israel's eastern neighbors, the Ammonites and Moabites (23:3). These restrictions will be lifted in the messianic age (Is 56:4–8).

23:2 bastard: Or, possibly, "child of incest".

23:3 Ammonite or Moabite: Distant relatives of the Israelites who dwelt east of the Dead Sea (2:9, 19). According to Genesis, both peoples were born of incest (Gen 19:30–38).

23:4 Balaam: A Mesopotamian sorcerer hired to curse Israel. See note on Num 22:5.

23:7 Edomite: A descendant of Esau. See note on 2:4.

23:10–14 Sanitation laws to protect the holiness of Israel's war camp. Soldiers must go outside the camp after a nocturnal emission of semen (23:10) and for defecation (23:13).

23:16 dwell with you: Runaway slaves from foreign lands are given refuge in Israel without fear of extradition.

23:17 no cult prostitute: Prohibits the Israelites from engaging in the impurities of the Canaanite cults of the land, which seem to have included sacred prostitution as a fertility rite. Unfortunately, failure to heed this law among the covenant people is documented (1 Kings 14:24; 2 Kings 23:7).

23:18 harlot: A female prostitute. **dog:** A male prostitute.

23:20 interest: Allows for the collection of interest on loans to Gentiles. Usury is still forbidden on assistance loans to fellow Israelites, as in earlier legislation (Ex 22:25). See note on 15:3.

23:21 a vow: A solemn promise freely made. For more on vows, see Lev 27 and Num 30.

---

r Ch 23:1 in Heb.
s Heb *uncover his father's skirt*.
t Or *male prostitute*.

has passed your lips, for you have voluntarily vowed to the Lord your God what you have promised with your mouth.

24 "When you go into your neighbor's vineyard, you may eat your fill of grapes, as many as you wish, but you shall not put any in your vessel. 25When you go into your neighbor's standing grain, you may pluck the ears with your hand, but you shall not put a sickle to your neighbor's standing grain.

Laws concerning Marriage and Divorce

24 * "When a man takes a wife and marries her, if then she finds no favor in his eyes because he has found some indecency in her, and he writes her a bill of divorce and puts it in her hand and sends her out of his house, and she departs out of his house, 2and if she goes and becomes another man's wife, 3and the latter husband dislikes her and writes her a bill of divorce and puts it in her hand and sends her out of his house, or if the latter husband dies, who took her to be his wife, 4then her former husband, who sent her away, may not take her again to be his wife, after she has been defiled; for that is an abomination before the Lord, and you shall not bring guilt upon the land which the Lord your God gives you for an inheritance.

Various Laws

5 "When a man is newly married, he shall not go out with the army or be charged with any business;

he shall be free at home one year, to be happy with his wife whom he has taken.

6 "No man shall take a mill or an upper millstone in pledge; for he would be taking a life in pledge.

7 "If a man is found stealing one of his brethren, the sons of Israel, and if he treats him as a slave or sells him, then that thief shall die; so you shall purge the evil from the midst of you.

8 "Take heed, in an attack of leprosy, to be very careful to do according to all that the Levitical priests shall direct you; as I commanded them, so you shall be careful to do. 9Remember what the Lord your God did to Miriam on the way as you came forth out of Egypt.

10 "When you make your neighbor a loan of any sort, you shall not go into his house to fetch his pledge. 11You shall stand outside, and the man to whom you make the loan shall bring the pledge out to you. 12And if he is a poor man, you shall not sleep in his pledge; 13when the sun goes down, you shall restore to him the pledge that he may sleep in his cloak and bless you; and it shall be righteousness to you before the Lord your God.

14 "You shall not oppress a hired servant who is poor and needy, whether he is one of your brethren or one of the sojourners who are in your land within your towns; 15you shall give him his hire on the day he earns it, before the sun goes down (for he is poor,

---

24:1: Mt 5:31; 19:7; Mk 10:4.   **24:6, 10–13**: Ex 22:26, 27.   **24:7**: Ex 21:16; 1 Cor 5:13.
24:8, 9: Lev 13–14.   **24:14, 15**: Lev 19:13; Jas 5:4.

23:24–25 Handfuls of a neighbor's crop may be picked and eaten, but harvesting is prohibited.

24:1–4 Deuteronomy prohibits a man from divorcing and remarrying the same woman if an intervening marriage (and divorce) has taken place. Without this restriction, a husband, who alone had the legal right to initiate divorce, could dismiss and remarry the same woman several times, making her a pawn at the mercy of his whims. Deuteronomy does not thereby throw open the doors to divorce; rather, it tolerates divorce as an existing practice (mentioned earlier in Lev 21:7, 14; 22:13; Num 30:9) and regulates it to limit abuses. • Jesus described divorce and remarriage as a legal concession to the sinfulness of Israel (Mt 19:8). But instead of reaffirming these practices, he revoked the Mosaic permission and restored the original standard of lifelong marriage that God instituted at creation (Mk 10:5–12; Lk 16:18) (CCC 1610).

24:1 indecency: The Hebrew (literally "nakedness of a thing") concerns the reason for divorce but is uncertain in meaning. Adultery is probably not intended, since an adulteress was put to death rather than divorced (22:22). In later Judaism, the legal ground for divorce was defined in various ways, from insubordination (Sir 25:25–26) to unchaste or immodest behavior (Rabbi Shammai) to the transfer of a husband's affection to another woman (Rabbi Akiba) to trivial matters displeasing to a husband, such as ruining a cooked meal (Rabbi Hillel). **bill of divorce:** A legal document ending

the marriage (Is 50:1). It may have included provisions for settlement money, as in other divorce documents of the ancient Near East.

24:4 defiled: I.e., by the second marriage. Use of this language elsewhere may imply that the woman has become defiled like an adulteress (Num 5:13–14, 20).

24:5 free at home: The groom is enjoying a one-year exemption from military and civil service. This law promotes strong marriages, allows couples to start a family, and helps to protect young brides from the grief of widowhood within the first year of marriage.

24:6 a mill: An essential tool for food preparation. Such necessities of life must not be used as collateral against the repayment of a loan. Otherwise, starvation could come before the loan is paid off.

24:7 stealing: Kidnapping to make a profit in slave trade is a capital crime (Ex 21:16).

24:8 leprosy: Presupposes knowledge of the leprosy laws in Lev 13–14.

24:9 Miriam: The older sister of Moses (Num 26:59). She was briefly afflicted with leprosy as a punishment for sin (Num 12:1–16).

24:10 neighbor a loan: Loans were normally made to the poor (Ex 22:25). Allowing the debtor to choose his own pledge (a promissory token of repayment) was a humane and compassionate way of guarding his dignity.

24:15 on the day: Wages for hired laborers must be handed out before the end of the workday. Withholding daily payment is tantamount to oppression (Lev 19:13; Mal 3:5; CCC 2409, 2434). **cry against you:** A plea for divine justice (Jas 5:4; CCC 1867).

---

*24:1: Divorce was permitted in Old Testament times on account of "hardness of heart"; Jesus, however, insists that it was not in the original plan of God (Mt 19:7–9).

and sets his heart upon it); lest he cry against you to the LORD, and it be sin in you.

16 "The fathers shall not be put to death for the children, nor shall the children be put to death for the fathers; every man shall be put to death for his own sin.

17 "You shall not pervert the justice due to the sojourner or to the fatherless, or take a widow's garment in pledge; ¹⁸but you shall remember that you were a slave in Egypt and the LORD your God redeemed you from there; therefore I command you to do this.

19 "When you reap your harvest in your field, and have forgotten a sheaf in the field, you shall not go back to get it; it shall be for the sojourner, the fatherless, and the widow; that the LORD your God may bless you in all the work of your hands. ²⁰When you beat your olive trees, you shall not go over the boughs again; it shall be for the sojourner, the fatherless, and the widow. ²¹When you gather the grapes of your vineyard, you shall not glean it afterward; it shall be for the sojourner, the fatherless, and the widow. ²²You shall remember that you were a slave in the land of Egypt; therefore I command you to do this.

25 "If there is a dispute between men, and they come into court, and the judges decide between them, acquitting the innocent and condemning the guilty, ²then if the guilty man deserves to be beaten, the judge shall cause him to lie down and be beaten in his presence with a number of stripes in proportion to his offense. ³Forty stripes may be given him, but not more; lest, if one should go on to beat him with more stripes than these, your brother be degraded in your sight.

4 "You shall not muzzle an ox when it treads out the grain.

Duty to a Brother's Widow

5 "If brothers dwell together, and one of them dies and has no son, the wife of the dead shall not be married outside the family to a stranger; her husband's brother shall go in to her, and take her as his wife, and perform the duty of a husband's brother to her. ⁶And the first son whom she bears shall succeed to the name of his brother who is dead, that his name may not be blotted out of Israel. ⁷And if the man does not wish to take his brother's wife, then his brother's wife shall go up to the gate to the elders, and say, 'My husband's brother refuses to perpetuate his brother's name in Israel; he will not perform the duty of a husband's brother to me.' ⁸Then the elders of his city shall call him, and speak to him: and if he persists, saying, 'I do not wish to take her,' ⁹then his brother's wife shall go up to him in the presence of the elders, and pull his sandal off his foot, and spit in his face; and she shall answer and say, 'So shall it be done to the man who does not build up his brother's house.' ¹⁰And the name of his house^u shall be called in Israel, The house of him that had his sandal pulled off.

Various Commands

11 "When men fight with one another, and the wife of the one draws near to rescue her husband from the hand of him who is beating him, and puts out her hand and seizes him by the private parts, ¹²then you shall cut off her hand; your eye shall have no pity.

13 "You shall not have in your bag two kinds of weights, a large and a small. ¹⁴You shall not have

---

24:17, 18: Ex 22:21–24; 23:9; Lev 19:33, 34.   **24:19–22:** Lev 19:9, 10; 23:22.   **25:4:** 1 Cor 9:9; 1 Tim 5:18.
25:5, 6: Mt 22:24; Mk 12:19; Lk 20:28.   **25:13–16:** Lev 19:35, 36.

24:16 his own sin: Felons rather than their families are held responsible for capital crimes (2 Kings 14:6). For the moral principle of individual guilt, see Ezek 18:1–32.

24:19–22 Gleaning laws require farmers and landowners to help feed the less fortunate (Ruth 2:1–23). Memories of hardship in Egypt provide the motivation for this form of charity (24:22).

25:1–3 Due process for criminal cases includes a trial before judges, a conviction or acquittal, and a sentence of punishment for the guilty. The severity of the sentence must correspond to the severity of the wrong. The limit is set at 40 lashes for a serious offense, lest flogging become excessive and undignified.

25:1 the judges: The local judicial council (16:18–20).

25:3 Forty stripes: Lowered to 39 lashes in later times to safeguard against miscounting and potential abuse (2 Cor 11:24).

25:4 shall not muzzle: A working ox is allowed to eat from the grain he is processing. Humane treatment of animals is implied here as elsewhere in the book (22:6–7).
• Paul draws a spiritual lesson from this passage: Christian

clergy have a right to compensation for their labor (1 Cor 9:9; 1 Tim 5:18).

25:5–10 The law of levirate marriage (the Latin *levir* means "brother-in-law"). Though strictly optional, it urges a man to marry his brother's widow in the event that his brother dies without children. The purpose of the new union is to produce a son who will carry on the name of the deceased brother and will inherit his estate. Refusal to marry the widow is met with a ritual of public disgrace (25:9) and results in a shameful reputation (25:10). The duty of the brother-in-law, here codified as law, already had the force of custom in patriarchal times (Gen 38:8–11).

25:9 pull his sandal off: Removing the sandal is a symbolic legal action that removes any claim of the brother-in-law to inherit the deceased husband's estate. Some interpret the gesture as a curse of poverty.

25:11 seizes him: Assumes that the woman has injured the assailant's ability to father children.

25:13–16 A condemnation of dishonest business practices. Justice requires a fair use of weights and measures for all commercial transactions. The standard of measurement used for buying must be the same standard used for selling (Lev 19:35–36) (CCC 2409).

---

^uHeb *its name.*

in your house two kinds of measures, a large and a small. ¹⁵A full and just weight you shall have, a full and just measure you shall have; that your days may be prolonged in the land which the Lᴏʀᴅ your God gives you. ¹⁶For all who do such things, all who act dishonestly, are an abomination to the Lᴏʀᴅ your God.

17 "Remember what Am′alek did to you on the way as you came out of Egypt, ¹⁸how he attacked you on the way, when you were faint and weary, and cut off at your rear all who lagged behind you; and he did not fear God. ¹⁹Therefore when the Lᴏʀᴅ your God has given you rest from all your enemies round about, in the land which the Lᴏʀᴅ your God gives you for an inheritance to possess, you shall blot out the remembrance of Am′alek from under heaven; you shall not forget.

First Fruits and Tithes

26 "When you come into the land which the Lᴏʀᴅ your God gives you for an inheritance, and have taken possession of it, and live in it, ²you shall take some of the first of all the fruit of the ground, which you harvest from your land that the Lᴏʀᴅ your God gives you, and you shall put it in a basket, and you shall go to the place which the Lᴏʀᴅ your God will choose, to make his name to dwell there. ³And you shall go to the priest who is in office at that time, and say to him, 'I declare this day to the Lᴏʀᴅ your God that I have come into the land which the Lᴏʀᴅ swore to our fathers to give us.' ⁴Then the priest shall take the basket from your hand, and set it down before the altar of the Lᴏʀᴅ your God.

5 "And you shall make response before the Lᴏʀᴅ your God, 'A wandering Arame′an was my father; and he went down into Egypt and sojourned there, few in number; and there he became a nation, great, mighty, and populous. ⁶And the Egyptians treated us harshly, and afflicted us, and laid upon us hard bondage. ⁷Then we cried to the Lᴏʀᴅ the God of our fathers, and the Lᴏʀᴅ heard our voice, and saw our affliction, our toil, and our oppression; ⁸and the

Lᴏʀᴅ brought us out of Egypt with a mighty hand and an outstretched arm, with great terror, with signs and wonders; ⁹and he brought us into this place and gave us this land, a land flowing with milk and honey. ¹⁰And behold, now I bring the first of the fruit of the ground, which you, O Lᴏʀᴅ, have given me.' And you shall set it down before the Lᴏʀᴅ your God, and worship before the Lᴏʀᴅ your God; ¹¹and you shall rejoice in all the good which the Lᴏʀᴅ your God has given to you and to your house, you, and the Levite, and the sojourner who is among you.

12 "When you have finished paying all the tithe of your produce in the third year, which is the year of tithing, giving it to the Levite, the sojourner, the fatherless, and the widow, that they may eat within your towns and be filled, ¹³then you shall say before the Lᴏʀᴅ your God, 'I have removed the sacred portion out of my house, and moreover I have given it to the Levite, the sojourner, the fatherless, and the widow, according to all your commandment which you have commanded me; I have not transgressed any of your commandments, neither have I forgotten them; ¹⁴I have not eaten of the tithe while I was mourning, or removed any of it while I was unclean, or offered any of it to the dead; I have obeyed the voice of the Lᴏʀᴅ my God, I have done according to all that you have commanded me. ¹⁵Look down from your holy habitation, from heaven, and bless your people Israel and the ground which you have given us, as you swore to our fathers, a land flowing with milk and honey.'

Concluding Exhortation

16 "This day the Lᴏʀᴅ your God commands you to do these statutes and ordinances; you shall therefore be careful to do them with all your heart and with all your soul. ¹⁷You have declared this day concerning the Lᴏʀᴅ that he is your God, and that you will walk in his ways, and keep his statutes and his commandments and his ordinances, and will obey his voice; ¹⁸and the Lᴏʀᴅ has declared this day concerning you that you are a people for

---

25:17–19: Ex 17:14; 1 Sam 15.　**26:1–11:** Ex 22:29; 23:19; 34:26; Num 18:12, 13.

25:17 Amalek: Father of the Amalekites, who attacked the caravans of Israel fleeing the slavery of Egypt (Ex 17:8–13). Since that time, they have been sworn enemies of Israel (Ex 17:14–16; Num 24:20). Amalek himself is said to descend from Jacob's brother, Esau (Gen 36:12).

25:19 blot out: In later times, Saul will wage a campaign against the Amalekites (1 Sam 15:1–9), and David will finish the job of conquering them (2 Sam 8:11–12).

26:2 first of all the fruit: Not the first-fruits offering of 18:4, which is a yearly obligation, but a one-time tribute in gratitude for the land of Canaan. **the place:** The location of Israel's central sanctuary. See note on 12:5.

26:5–11 A confession of Israel's faith in the Lord, the great Redeemer from bondage and Giver of the Promised Land. See the similar confession, in a question-and-answer format, at 6:20–24.

26:5 wandering Aramean: The patriarch Jacob, whose mother, Rebekah, was an Aramean (Gen 25:20; 28:5).

His reputation as a wanderer is borne out by the stories in Genesis, which document Jacob's move to Paddan-aram in Syria (Gen 28:1–2; 29:1), his flight back to Canaan (Gen 31:17–21), and his migration to Egypt (Gen 46:5–6). **a nation, great:** In fulfillment of the promise made to Abraham (Gen 12:2; 17:2).

26:12 the tithe: The triennial tithe collected for the Levites and the needy (14:28–29).

26:14 while I was unclean: Handling the tithe in a state of ritual impurity would have defiled it, so that it no longer served as a holy offering. **to the dead:** Food offerings to idols are meant.

26:15 your holy habitation: The sanctuary of heaven, where the Lord dwells in glory and looks down upon his people (1 Kings 8:30).

26:16–19 The Lord and Israel declare their intent to adhere to the covenant of Deuteronomy. Israel's promise will be upgraded into sworn oaths, as stipulated in 27:12–26.

his own possession, as he has promised you, and that you are to keep all his commandments, ¹⁹that he will set you high above all nations that he has made, in praise and in fame and in honor, and that you shall be a people holy to the Lord your God, as he has spoken."

The Inscribed Stones and Altar on Mount Ebal

27 Now Moses and the elders of Israel commanded the people, saying, "Keep all the commandment which I command you this day. ²And on the day you pass over the Jordan to the land which the Lord your God gives you, you shall set up large stones, and plaster them with plaster; ³and you shall write upon them all the words of this law, when you pass over to enter the land which the Lord your God gives you, a land flowing with milk and honey, as the Lord, the God of your fathers, has promised you. ⁴And when you have passed over the Jordan, you shall set up these stones, concerning which I command you this day, on Mount E'bal, and you shall plaster them with plaster. ⁵And there you shall build an altar to the Lord your God, an altar of stones; you shall lift up no iron tool upon them. ⁶You shall build an altar to the Lord your God of unhewn ᵛ stones; and you shall offer burnt offerings on it to the Lord your God; ⁷and you shall sacrifice peace offerings, and shall eat there; and you shall rejoice before the Lord your God. ⁸And you shall write upon the stones all the words of this law very plainly."

9 And Moses and the Levitical priests said to all Israel, "Keep silence and hear, O Israel: this day you have become the people of the Lord your God. ¹⁰You shall therefore obey the voice of the Lord your God, keeping his commandments and his statutes, which I command you this day."

Twelve Curses at Mount Ebal

11 And Moses charged the people the same day, saying, ¹²"When you have passed over the Jordan, these shall stand upon Mount Ger'izim to bless the people: Simeon, Levi, Judah, Is'sachar, Joseph, and Benjamin. ¹³And these shall stand upon Mount E'bal for the curse: Reuben, Gad, Asher, Zeb'ulun, Dan, and Naph'tali. ¹⁴And the Levites shall declare to all the men of Israel with a loud voice:

15 "'Cursed be the man who makes a graven or molten image, an abomination to the Lord, a thing made by the hands of a craftsman, and sets it up in secret.' And all the people shall answer and say, 'Amen.'

16 "'Cursed be he who dishonors his father or his mother.' And all the people shall say, 'Amen.'

17 "'Cursed be he who removes his neighbor's landmark.' And all the people shall say, 'Amen.'

18 "'Cursed be he who misleads a blind man on the road.' And all the people shall say, 'Amen.'

19 "'Cursed be he who perverts the justice due to the sojourner, the fatherless, and the widow.' And all the people shall say, 'Amen.'

27:15: Ex 20:4, 23; 34:17; Lev 19:4; 26:1; Deut 4:16, 23, 25; 5:8; 7:25.   **27:16:** Ex 20:12; 21:15, 17; Lev 20:9; Deut 5:16; 21:18–21.   **27:18:** Lev 19:14.   **27:19:** Ex 22:21–24; 23:9; Lev 19:33, 34; Deut 24:17, 18.

📖 **27:1–26** Procedures for the ratification of the Deuteronomic covenant, which will take place at Shechem in Josh 8:30–35. In many ways, the Shechem liturgy of Deut 27 mirrors the Sinai liturgy of Ex 24: both take place at a mountain (27:4; Ex 19:2), and both involve memorial stones (27:2; Ex 24:4), an inscription of the law (27:3; Ex 24:4), the building of an altar (27:5; Ex 24:4), the sacrifice of burnt offerings and peace offerings (27:6–7; Ex 24:5), and a ratification meal (27:7; Ex 24:11). However, there are important differences: this covenant **(1)** is made with the children of the Exodus generation rather than their parents, who came out of Egypt, **(2)** includes no theophany or sensible manifestation of the Lord's glory and power, and **(3)** requires the people to inscribe the law on stone monuments instead of God himself writing it on stone tablets. Differences such as these reinforce the claim in 29:1 that the Deuteronomic covenant (on the plains of Moab) is distinct from the Sinai covenant (at Horeb).

27:2 large stones: Turned upright as memorials and coated with plaster to receive writing. It was common practice in the Near East to record covenant stipulations and law codes on stone slabs and steles.

27:4 Mount Ebal: One of two mountains, along with Mt. Gerizim, that rise next to the city of Shechem in central Israel. The Samaritan Pentateuch reads differently in this passage, giving the location of the ceremony as Gerizim rather than Ebal.

27:5 no iron tool: Altar stones must be rough and unhewn (Ex 20:25). This contrasts with the idol altars of Canaan, which archaeology shows to have been made of dressed stones neatly cut and fitted together.

27:11–14 The tribes will assemble on the slopes of Ebal and Gerizim, pledging themselves to the Lord and invoking the blessings and curses of the covenant (listed in Deut 28). Gerizim, the southern peak, will host the six tribes of central and southern Israel (27:12). Ebal, the northern peak, will host the six tribes of northern Israel and the Transjordan (27:13).

27:14 the Levites: Israel's ministers of worship, who will stand in the valley between Ebal and Gerizim bearing the Ark of the Covenant (Josh 8:33). The rest of the tribe of Levi will join the lay tribes standing on Gerizim (27:12).

27:15–26 A litany of twelve curses invoked by the twelve tribes. These are oaths of loyalty that ratify the Deuteronomic covenant. The priests will administer the oaths (27:14) as the people swear their allegiance to the Lord with the antiphonal refrain, "Amen" (27:15, 16, 17, etc.). The nature of these curses is not specified here, only the sins that trigger them. The covenant curses are listed in 28:15–68.

27:15 graven ... image: A transgression of the first commandment (5:6–10). **Amen:** A Hebrew acclamation, meaning, "so be it". It is a way of giving assent to an oath (Num 5:22).

27:16 dishonors his father: A transgression of the fourth commandment (5:16).

27:17 landmark: A transgression of the property law in 19:14.

ᵛ Heb *whole*.

20 "'Cursed be he who lies with his father's wife, because he has uncovered her who is his father's.'ᵂ And all the people shall say, 'Amen.'

21 "'Cursed be he who lies with any kind of beast.' And all the people shall say, 'Amen.'

22 "'Cursed be he who lies with his sister, whether the daughter of his father or the daughter of his mother.' And all the people shall say, 'Amen.'

23 "'Cursed be he who lies with his mother-in-law.' And all the people shall say, 'Amen.'

24 "'Cursed be he who slays his neighbor in secret.' And all the people shall say, 'Amen.'

25 "'Cursed be he who takes a bribe to slay an innocent person.' And all the people shall say, 'Amen.'

26 "'Cursed be he who does not confirm the words of this law by doing them.' And all the people shall say, 'Amen.'

Blessing for Obedience

28 "And if you obey the voice of the LORD your God, being careful to do all his commandments which I command you this day, the LORD your God will set you high above all the nations of the earth. ²And all these blessings shall come upon you and overtake you, if you obey the voice of the LORD your God. ³Blessed shall you be in the city, and blessed shall you be in the field. ⁴Blessed shall be the fruit of your body, and the fruit of your ground, and the fruit of your beasts, the increase of your cattle, and the young of your flock. ⁵Blessed shall be your basket and your kneading-trough. ⁶Blessed shall you be when you come in, and blessed shall you be when you go out.

7 "The LORD will cause your enemies who rise against you to be defeated before you; they shall come out against you one way, and flee before you seven ways. ⁸The LORD will command the blessing upon you in your barns, and in all that you undertake; and he will bless you in the land which the LORD your God gives you. ⁹The LORD will establish you as a people holy to himself, as he has sworn to you, if you keep the commandments of the LORD your God, and walk in his ways. ¹⁰And all the peoples of the earth shall see that you are called by the name of the LORD; and they shall be afraid of you. ¹¹And the LORD will make you abound in prosperity, in the fruit of your body, and in the fruit of your cattle, and in the fruit of your ground, within the land which the LORD swore to your fathers to give you. ¹²The LORD will open to you his good treasury the heavens, to give the rain of your land in its season and to bless all the work of your hands; and you shall lend to many nations, but you shall not borrow. ¹³And the LORD will make you the head, and not the tail; and you shall tend upward only, and not downward; if you obey the commandments of the LORD your God, which I command you this day, being careful to do them, ¹⁴and if you do not turn aside from any of the words which I command you this day, to the right hand or to the left, to go after other gods to serve them.

Warnings against Disobedience

15 "But if you will not obey the voice of the LORD your God or be careful to do all his commandments and his statutes which I command you this day, then all these curses shall come upon you and

---

27:20: Lev 18:8; 20:11; Deut 22:30.   **27:21:** Ex 22:19; Lev 18:23; 20:15.   **27:22:** Lev 18:9; 20:17.
27:23: Lev 18:17; 20:14.   **27:26:** Gal 3:10.   **28:** Lev 26:3–45.

27:20 father's wife: A stepmother (Lev 18:8).

27:21 any kind of beast: A transgression of the law against bestiality in Lev 18:23.

27:22 sister: A stepsister or half-sister (Lev 18:9).

27:24 slays his neighbor: A transgression of the fifth commandment (5:17).

27:25 takes a bribe: A transgression of the law in 16:19.

27:26 words of this law: The final curse is climactic and comprehensive, applying to any infraction of the Mosaic Law not specified in the preceding list. • Paul cites this final curse in Gal 3:10 to insist that embracing the Mosaic Law is tantamount to triggering its curses, since no one can observe all of its precepts without fault. Jesus redeemed us from the curse of the Law when he died for the sins of the world (Gal 3:13).

28:1–68 The sanctions of the Deuteronomic covenant, i.e., the *blessings* that come as rewards for obedience (28:1–14) and the *curses* that come as punishments on disobedience (28:15–68). Both possibilities are conditional, as indicated by the "if" in 28:1 and 28:15. Blessings and curses likewise appear in ancient Near Eastern treaties and law codes from the second millennium B.C. (Hittite vassal treaties, the *Code of Hammurabi*, the *Laws of Lipit-Ishtar*). A few of the curses

in Deut 28 find parallels in first-millennium texts from Assyria (*Vassal Treaties of Esarhaddon*).

28:1 above all the nations: Envisions the preeminence of Israel as a world power and ruler in the Near East. Israel lived at this political height only briefly during the kingship of David and Solomon (2 Sam 22:44; 1 Kings 4:21; Ps 89:27).

28:2 these blessings: The divine favors poured out upon families, flocks, and fields (28:4) and manifest in abundant fertility (28:11), food supplies (28:5, 8), and financial wealth (28:12).

28:6 come in ... go out: Refers to daily activities and endeavors (Ps 121:8).

28:9 holy to himself: Set apart for the Lord and his sacred purposes. See note on Ex 19:6.

28:12 lend to many: Evidence of economic prosperity. Beyond that, commercial interest loans to foreigners would increase wealth in Israel still more (23:20).

28:13 the head: The ruler of other nations (15:6; 28:1).

28:15 these curses: The divine chastisements of destruction (28:20), disease (28:27, 35, 59–61), drought (28:22–24), defeat (28:25, 48–57), death (28:26), dementia (28:28), dispossession (28:29–34), domination (28:36), devastation of crops (28:39–40, 42), decreased population (28:62), and, ultimately, deportation into exile (28:37, 41) and dispersion among the nations (28:64–68). Several of the curses in 28:15–68 are mirror opposites of the blessings in 28:1–14.

ᵂHeb *uncovered his father's skirt.*

overtake you. ¹⁶Cursed shall you be in the city, and cursed shall you be in the field. ¹⁷Cursed shall be your basket and your kneading-trough. ¹⁸Cursed shall be the fruit of your body, and the fruit of your ground, the increase of your cattle, and the young of your flock. ¹⁹Cursed shall you be when you come in, and cursed shall you be when you go out.

20 "The Lᴏʀᴅ will send upon you curses, confusion, and frustration, in all that you undertake to do, until you are destroyed and perish quickly, on account of the evil of your doings, because you have forsaken me. ²¹The Lᴏʀᴅ will make the pestilence cling to you until he has consumed you off the land which you are entering to take possession of it. ²²The Lᴏʀᴅ will strike you with consumption, and with fever, inflammation, and fiery heat, and with drought,* and with blasting, and with mildew; they shall pursue you until you perish. ²³And the heavens over your head shall be brass, and the earth under you shall be iron. ²⁴The Lᴏʀᴅ will make the rain of your land powder and dust; from heaven it shall come down upon you until you are destroyed.

25 "The Lᴏʀᴅ will cause you to be defeated before your enemies; you shall go out one way against them, and flee seven ways before them; and you shall be a horror to all the kingdoms of the earth. ²⁶And your dead body shall be food for all birds of the air, and for the beasts of the earth; and there shall be no one to frighten them away. ²⁷The Lᴏʀᴅ will strike you with the boils of Egypt, and with the ulcers and the scurvy and the itch, of which you cannot be healed. ²⁸The Lᴏʀᴅ will strike you with madness and blindness and confusion of mind; ²⁹and you shall grope at noonday, as the blind grope in darkness, and you shall not prosper in your ways; and you shall be only oppressed and robbed continually, and there shall be no one to help you. ³⁰You shall betroth a wife, and another man shall lie with her; you shall build a house, and you shall not dwell in it; you shall plant a vineyard, and you shall not use the fruit of it. ³¹Your ox shall be slain before your eyes, and you shall not eat of it; your donkey shall be violently taken away before your face, and shall not be restored to you; your sheep shall be given to your enemies, and there shall be no one to help you. ³²Your sons and your daughters shall be given to another people, while your eyes look on and fail with longing for them all the day; and it shall not be in the power of your hand to prevent it. ³³A nation which you have not known shall eat up the fruit of your ground and of all your labors; and you shall be only oppressed and crushed continually; ³⁴so that you shall be driven mad by the sight which your eyes shall see. ³⁵The Lᴏʀᴅ will strike you on the knees and on the legs with grievous boils of which you cannot be healed, from the sole of your foot to the crown of your head.

36 "The Lᴏʀᴅ will bring you, and your king whom you set over you, to a nation that neither you nor your fathers have known; and there you shall serve other gods, of wood and stone. ³⁷And you shall become a horror, a proverb, and a byword, among all the peoples where the Lᴏʀᴅ will lead you away. ³⁸You shall carry much seed into the field, and shall gather little in; for the locust shall consume it. ³⁹You shall plant vineyards and dress them, but you shall neither drink of the wine nor gather the grapes; for the worm shall eat them. ⁴⁰You shall have olive trees throughout all your territory, but you shall not anoint yourself with the oil; for your olives shall drop off. ⁴¹You shall beget sons and daughters, but they shall not be yours; for they shall go into captivity. ⁴²All your trees and the fruit of your ground the locust shall possess. ⁴³The sojourner who is among you shall mount above you higher and higher; and you shall come down lower and lower. ⁴⁴He shall lend to you, and you shall not lend to him; he shall be the head, and you shall be the tail. ⁴⁵All these curses shall come upon you and pursue you and overtake you, till you are destroyed, because you did not obey the voice of the Lᴏʀᴅ your God, to keep his commandments and his statutes which he commanded you. ⁴⁶They shall be upon you as a sign and a wonder, and upon your descendants for ever.

47 "Because you did not serve the Lᴏʀᴅ your God with joyfulness and gladness of heart, by reason of the abundance of all things, ⁴⁸therefore you shall serve your enemies whom the Lᴏʀᴅ will send against you, in hunger and thirst, in nakedness, and in want of all things; and he will put a yoke of iron upon your neck, until he has destroyed you. ⁴⁹The

---

28:49: 1 Cor 14:21.

28:23 brass ... iron: Similar imagery occurs in Lev 26:19.

28:26 your dead body: Israel, like an unburied corpse, will provide a feast for scavengers and carnivores (Jer 7:33; Mt 24:28).

28:30 wife ... house ... vineyard: A curse that takes away the anticipated joys of the newlywed, the new homeowner, and the farmer (20:5-7).

28:33 A nation: A foreign invader that will come to devastate Israel (28:36, 49).

28:36 your king: The monarch envisioned in 17:14-15.

28:38 the locust: Evokes memories of the locust plague in Egypt (Ex 10:12-15) and anticipates the locust judgment that will ravage Israel in the days of the prophet Joel (Joel 1:1-4).

28:49 the eagle: The nation sent by the Lord to administer the curse of military conquest on sinful Israel. Historically, this role was fulfilled by the Assyrians in the eight century B.C. (Hos 8:1, translated "vulture"), the Babylonians in the sixth century B.C. (Hab 1:8), and the Romans in the first century A.D. (Mt 24:28). See note on 28:64. **language:** The foreign tongues of the invaders, namely, the East Semitic dialects of Assyria and Babylon and the classical Latin of the Romans (Is 28:11-13; Jer 5:15).

---

*Another reading is *sword*.

LORD will bring a nation against you from afar, from the end of the earth, as swift as the eagle flies, a nation whose language you do not understand, [50]a nation of stern countenance, who shall not regard the person of the old or show favor to the young, [51]and shall eat the offspring of your cattle and the fruit of your ground, until you are destroyed; who also shall not leave you grain, wine, or oil, the increase of your cattle or the young of your flock, until they have caused you to perish. [52]They shall besiege you in all your towns, until your high and fortified walls, in which you trusted, come down throughout all your land; and they shall besiege you in all your towns throughout all your land, which the LORD your God has given you. [53]And you shall eat the offspring of your own body, the flesh of your sons and daughters, whom the LORD your God has given you, in the siege and in the distress with which your enemies shall distress you. [54]The man who is the most tender and delicately bred among you will grudge food to his brother, to the wife of his bosom, and to the last of the children who remain to him; [55]so that he will not give to any of them any of the flesh of his children whom he is eating, because he has nothing left him, in the siege and in the distress with which your enemy shall distress you in all your towns. [56]The most tender and delicately bred woman among you, who would not venture to set the sole of her foot upon the ground because she is so delicate and tender, will grudge to the husband of her bosom, to her son and to her daughter, [57]her afterbirth that comes out from between her feet and her children whom she bears, because she will eat them secretly, for want of all things, in the siege and in the distress with which your enemy shall distress you in your towns.

58 "If you are not careful to do all the words of this law which are written in this book, that you may fear this glorious and awesome name, the LORD your God, [59]then the LORD will bring on you and your offspring extraordinary afflictions, afflictions severe and lasting, and sicknesses grievous and lasting. [60]And he will bring upon you again all the diseases of Egypt, which you were afraid of; and they shall cling to you. [61]Every sickness also, and every affliction which is not recorded in the book of this law, the LORD will bring upon you, until you are destroyed. [62]Whereas you were as the stars of heaven for multitude, you shall be left few in number; because you did not obey the voice of the LORD your God. [63]And as the LORD took delight in doing you good and multiplying you, so the LORD will take delight in bringing ruin upon you and destroying you; and you shall be plucked off the land which you are entering to take possession of it. [64]And the LORD will scatter you among all peoples, from one end of the earth to the other; and there you shall serve other gods, of wood and stone, which neither you nor your fathers have known. [65]And among these nations you shall find no ease, and there shall be no rest for the sole of your foot; but the LORD will give you there a trembling heart, and failing eyes, and a languishing soul; [66]your life shall hang in doubt before you; night and day you shall be in dread, and have no assurance of your life. [67]In the morning you shall say, 'Would it were evening!' and at evening you shall say, 'Would it were morning!' because of the dread which your heart shall fear, and the sights which your eyes shall see. [68]And the LORD will bring you back in ships to Egypt, a journey which I promised that you should never make again; and there you shall offer yourselves for sale to your enemies as male and female slaves, but no man will buy you."

The Covenant Renewed in Moab

29 [y]These are the words of the covenant which the LORD commanded Moses to make with the sons of Israel in the land of Moab, besides the covenant which he had made with them at Horeb.

28:53 eat the offspring: In times of siege, when food supplies are cut off, men and women will become like beasts feeding on the flesh of their loved ones. Cannibalism is the ultimate act of desperation in the fight against starvation (2 Kings 6:24–29; Jer 19:9).

28:60 diseases of Egypt: Perhaps a reference to the plague of boils and sores (Ex 9:9; 15:26).

28:62 few in number: Israel will suffer casualties on such a grand scale that its population will be whittled down to a bare remnant of survivors. For a historical fulfillment of this threat, see Is 10:22.

28:64 scatter you: The curse of exile. It will become a reality when the Assyrians conquer the Northern Kingdom of Israel in the eighth century B.C. (2 Kings 17:2), when the Babylonians sack the Southern Kingdom of Judah in the sixth century B.C. (2 Kings 25:1–11), and again when the Romans conquer Jeru-

salem and Judea in the first century A.D. (Lk 21:20–24). See note on 28:49.

28:68 ships: Galley ships used for slave trade on the Mediterranean. **Egypt:** Implies that Israel will be re-enslaved by Gentiles.

29:1 These are the words: Refers to the laws in chaps. 5–26 as well as the blessings and curses in chaps. 27–28. This is clear in the Hebrew text, where 29:1 is the closing verse of chap. 28 (see textual note y). **the covenant:** The Deuteronomic covenant is distinct from the Sinai covenant, the two being made at different *times*, in different *places*, and with different *people*. The Sinai covenant was ratified at Horeb in the first year of the Exodus with the generation of Israelites who were freed from slavery. The Deuteronomic covenant, by contrast, is made on the plains of Moab in the fortieth year of the Exodus with the children of the generation that came forth from Egypt. See note on 27:1–26. **Moab:** The elevated plain northeast of the Dead Sea. Here, at a place called Shittim, Israel made its final encampment (Num 22:1) before crossing the Jordan into Canaan (Josh 3:1–17). **besides:** Or "in addition to". **Horeb:** Another name for Sinai.

---

y Ch 28:69 in Heb.

2 ᶻ And Moses summoned all Israel and said to them: "You have seen all that the Lᴏʀᴅ did before your eyes in the land of Egypt, to Pharaoh and to all his servants and to all his land, ³the great trials which your eyes saw, the signs, and those great wonders; ⁴but to this day the Lᴏʀᴅ has not given you a mind to understand, or eyes to see, or ears to hear. ⁵I have led you forty years in the wilderness; your clothes have not worn out upon you, and your sandals have not worn off your feet; ⁶you have not eaten bread, and you have not drunk wine or strong drink; that you may know that I am the Lᴏʀᴅ your God. ⁷And when you came to this place, Si'hon the king of Heshbon and Og the king of Bashan came out against us to battle, but we defeated them; ⁸we took their land, and gave it for an inheritance to the Reubenites, the Gadites, and the half-tribe of the Manas'sites. ⁹Therefore be careful to do the words of this covenant, that you may prosperᵃ in all that you do.

10 "You stand this day all of you before the Lᴏʀᴅ your God; the heads of your tribes,ᵇ your elders, and your officers, all the men of Israel, ¹¹your little ones, your wives, and the sojourner who is in your camp, both he who hews your wood and he who draws your water, ¹²that you may enter into the sworn covenant of the Lᴏʀᴅ your God, which the Lᴏʀᴅ your God makes with you this day; ¹³that he may establish you this day as his people, and that he may be your God, as he promised you, and as he swore to your fathers, to Abraham, to Isaac, and to Jacob. ¹⁴Nor is it with you only that I make this sworn covenant, ¹⁵but with him who is not here with us this day as well as with him who stands here with us this day before the Lᴏʀᴅ our God.

16 "You know how we dwelt in the land of Egypt, and how we came through the midst of the nations through which you passed; ¹⁷and you have seen their detestable things, their idols of wood and stone, of silver and gold, which were among them. ¹⁸Beware lest there be among you a man or woman or family or tribe, whose heart turns away this day from the Lᴏʀᴅ our God to go and serve the gods of those nations; lest there be among you a root bearing poisonous and bitter fruit, ¹⁹one who, when he hears the words of this sworn covenant, blesses himself in his heart, saying, 'I shall be safe, though I walk in the stubbornness of my heart.' This would lead to the sweeping away of moist and dry alike. ²⁰The Lᴏʀᴅ would not pardon him, but rather the anger of the Lᴏʀᴅ and his jealousy would smoke against that man, and the curses written in this book would settle upon him, and the Lᴏʀᴅ would blot out his name from under heaven. ²¹And the Lᴏʀᴅ would single him out from all the tribes of Israel for calamity, in accordance with all the curses of the covenant written in this book of the law. ²²And the generation to come, your children who rise up after you, and the foreigner who comes from a far land, would say, when they see the afflictions of that land and the sicknesses with which the Lᴏʀᴅ has made it sick—²³the whole land brimstone and salt, and a burnt-out waste, unsown, and growing nothing, where no grass can sprout, an overthrow like that of Sodom and Gomor'rah, Admah and Zeboi'im, which the Lᴏʀᴅ overthrew in his anger and wrath—²⁴yes, all the nations would say, 'Why has the Lᴏʀᴅ done thus to this land? What means the heat of this great anger?' ²⁵Then men would say, 'It is because they forsook the covenant of the Lᴏʀᴅ, the God of their fathers, which he made with them when he brought them out of the land of Egypt, ²⁶and went and served other gods and worshiped them, gods whom they had not known and whom he had not allotted to them; ²⁷therefore the anger of the Lᴏʀᴅ was kindled against this land, bringing upon it all the curses written in this book; ²⁸and the Lᴏʀᴅ uprooted them from their land in anger and fury

---

29:4: Rom 11:8. **29:18**: Acts 8:23; Heb 12:15.

29:3 your eyes saw: The assembly listening to Moses would have been children or teens when they witnessed the marvels of the Exodus. Everyone over 19 years old at that time had since perished before Moses spoke these words (2:14; Num 14:26–35).

29:4 eyes to see ... ears to hear: An idiom for spiritual discernment. Moses contends that Israel lacks a right understanding of divine revelation as well as a right perception of its own spiritual needs. Failing to recognize the need for grace, the people failed to ask for it (Jas 4:2). This would not be the first time Israel proved to be blind and deaf to the word of the Lord (Is 6:9–10; Jer 5:21; Ezek 12:2).

29:7 defeated them: The conquest of the Transjordan (Num 21:21–35).

29:9 prosper: I.e., enjoy the blessings of the covenant (28:1–14).

29:11 hews ... draws: Later associated with a state of vassalage (Josh 9:21).

29:12 sworn covenant: The oaths sworn to ratify the Deuteronomic covenant are expressed in the "Amen" antiphons of 27:15–26.

29:15 who is not here: The Deuteronomic covenant extends beyond the Israel of Moses' day to include future generations.

29:19 moist and dry alike: A metaphor for complete destruction, suggesting that violators of the covenant will trigger divine judgments that affect everyone, faithful and faithless alike.

29:20 the curses: Written down in 28:15–68.

29:23 Sodom ... Zeboiim: Four wicked cities that once existed near the Dead Sea (Gen 14:2). In Abraham's day, God destroyed them with the fire and brimstone of his wrath (Gen 19:24–29). The land of Israel will suffer similar devastation if it turns away from the Lord to serve idols (29:18).

ᶻCh 29:1 in Heb.
ᵃOr *deal wisely.*
ᵇGk Syr: Heb *your heads, your tribes.*

and great wrath, and cast them into another land, as at this day.'

29 "The secret things belong to the LORD our God; but the things that are revealed belong to us and to our children for ever, that we may do all the words of this law.

God's Fidelity Assured

30 "And when all these things come upon you, the blessing and the curse, which I have set before you, and you call them to mind among all the nations where the LORD your God has driven you, ²and return to the LORD your God, you and your children, and obey his voice in all that I command you this day, with all your heart and with all your soul; ³then the LORD your God will restore your fortunes, and have compassion upon you, and he will gather you again from all the peoples where the LORD your God has scattered you. ⁴If your outcasts are in the uttermost parts of heaven, from there the LORD your God will gather you, and from there he will fetch you; ⁵and the LORD your God will bring you into the land which your fathers possessed, that you may possess it; and he will make you more prosperous and numerous than your fathers. ⁶And the LORD your God will circumcise your heart and the heart of your offspring, so that you will love the LORD your God with all your heart and with all your soul, that you may live. ⁷And the LORD your God will put all these curses upon your foes and enemies who persecuted you. ⁸And you shall again obey the voice of the LORD, and keep all his commandments which I command you this day. ⁹The LORD your God will make you abundantly prosperous in all the work of your hand, in the fruit of your body, and in the fruit of your cattle, and in the fruit of your ground; for the LORD will again take delight in prospering you, as he took delight in your fathers, ¹⁰if you

---

30:4: Mt 24:31; Mk 13:27.

29:29 secret things: The unknowns of the future. Since these belong to the Lord, Israel need only concern itself with following the commandments made known through Moses.

30:1–10 Moses foresees the rebellion, repentance, and restoration of Israel. **(1)** Rebellion will bring a curse of exile that scatters Israel among many nations. **(2)** Repentance will come when Israel, humbled and disciplined by the curse, turns back to the Lord with a new desire to love and obey him. **(3)** Restoration follows when God bestows mercy and blessings upon Israel. Moses envisions these future events as an inspired prophet (34:10).

30:1 when: The apostasy of Israel is a certainty rather than a mere possibility. Assurance of this tragic betrayal comes from the Lord, who revealed the future to Moses (31:16–18).

30:3 will gather you: The return of Jewish exiles from Babylon in the sixth century B.C. is a partial fulfillment of this promise (Ezra 1–2; Jer 29:10–14).

30:6 God will circumcise: Indicates that God will do for his people what they cannot do for themselves: cut away the stubbornness of the heart that resists his will (implied by the contrast with 10:16). Moses thus prophesies the divine work of grace within his people, a work that makes them newly responsive to the Lord. In the Greek LXX, the sentence reads: "the Lord will cleanse your heart." • Talk of a new circumcision implies the ratification of a new covenant. Just as circumcision of the flesh is an outward sign of the Abrahamic covenant (Gen 17:9–14), so also circumcision of the heart is an inward sign of the New Covenant sealed in messianic times (Rom 2:28–29). According to Paul, this is fulfilled by the renewal of the heart in Baptism, which he calls the "circumcision of Christ" (Col 2:11–12).

30:7 curses upon your foes: Recalls the Lord's promise that he will curse those who curse the family of Abraham (Gen 12:3; Num 24:9).

30:9 prosperous: The blessings of the covenant in 28:1–14 will again be enjoyed.

30:10 book of the law: Deuteronomy itself, which was written on a scroll and stored beside the Ark of the Covenant (31:24–26).

Word Study

Heart (30:6)

Lebab or *leb* (Heb.) means "heart" or "inner self". The noun appears hundreds of times in the OT. Occasionally it refers to the vital organ concealed in the chest (Ex 28:29; 2 Sam 18:14), but more often it denotes the whole interior of the person with all of its faculties and dimensions. The heart is the seat of wisdom (Prov 16:21), thought (Gen 6:5), feelings (Ex 4:14), memory (Ps 119:11), obedience (Prov 4:4), and the moral conscience (Job 27:6). It is the hidden center of the person that only God can see (1 Sam 16:7). It is also the place where man is most deeply wounded by sin (Gen 8:21; Jer 17:9). For this reason, the healing of the heart is a focal point of OT eschatology. Moses was the first to prophesy that God would perform spiritual circumcision on the rebellious heart of Israel, giving it a new power to love and obey him (Deut 30:6). Later Prophets only deepened this hope. Jeremiah foresees a new covenant with Israel in which the Lord writes his laws on the hearts of his people instead of on scrolls and tablets (Jer 31:31–34). Ezekiel describes this in terms of a heart transplant, in which the Lord replaces the stone hearts of his people with hearts of living flesh that respond to his love with obedience (Ezek 11:19–21; 36:26–27). Regardless of the metaphor used, the point is the same: the Lord must heal the heart of his people if they are to conquer their selfishness and walk in his ways (CCC 368).

obey the voice of the Lord your God, to keep his commandments and his statutes which are written in this book of the law, if you turn to the Lord your God with all your heart and with all your soul.

Exhortation to Choose Life

11 "For this commandment which I command you this day is not too hard for you, neither is it far off. ¹²It is not in heaven, that you should say, 'Who will go up for us to heaven, and bring it to us, that we may hear it and do it?' ¹³Neither is it beyond the sea, that you should say, 'Who will go over the sea for us, and bring it to us, that we may hear it and do it?' ¹⁴But the word is very near you; it is in your mouth and in your heart, so that you can do it.

15 "See, I have set before you this day life and good, death and evil. ¹⁶If you obey the commandments of the Lord your God ᶜ which I command you this day, by loving the Lord your God, by walking in his ways, and by keeping his commandments and his statutes and his ordinances, then you shall live and multiply, and the Lord your God will bless you in the land which you are entering to take possession of it. ¹⁷But if your heart turns away, and you will not hear, but are drawn away to worship other gods and serve them, ¹⁸I declare to you this day, that you shall perish; you shall not live long in the land which you are going over the Jordan to enter and possess. ¹⁹I call heaven and earth to witness against you this day, that I have set before you life and death, blessing and curse; therefore choose life, that you and your descendants may live, ²⁰loving the Lord

your God, obeying his voice, and clinging to him; for that means life to you and length of days, that you may dwell in the land which the Lord swore to your fathers, to Abraham, to Isaac, and to Jacob, to give them."

Joshua Becomes Moses' Successor

31 So Moses continued to speak these words to all Israel. ²And he said to them, "I am a hundred and twenty years old this day; I am no longer able to go out and come in. The Lord has said to me, 'You shall not go over this Jordan.' ³The Lord your God himself will go over before you; he will destroy these nations before you, so that you shall dispossess them; and Joshua will go over at your head, as the Lord has spoken. ⁴And the Lord will do to them as he did to Si'hon and Og, the kings of the Am'orites, and to their land, when he destroyed them. ⁵And the Lord will give them over to you, and you shall do to them according to all the commandment which I have commanded you. ⁶Be strong and of good courage, do not fear or be in dread of them: for it is the Lord your God who goes with you; he will not fail you or forsake you."

7 Then Moses summoned Joshua, and said to him in the sight of all Israel, "Be strong and of good courage; for you shall go with this people into the land which the Lord has sworn to their fathers to give them; and you shall put them in possession of it. ⁸It is the Lord who goes before you; he will be with you, he will not fail you or forsake you; do not fear or be dismayed."

30:12, 13: Rom 10:6, 7. **30:14:** Rom 10:8. **31:6, 8:** Heb 13:5.

30:11–14 Moses dismisses excuses for disobedience. Israel can neither claim ignorance of God's Law nor plead the inability to observe it. All is clearly revealed and made accessible to his people. What Israel lacks is the grace that comes through faith (29:4), and only faith in the Lord makes faithfulness to his Law a real possibility (Rom 9:30–32). • Paul applies this assessment of the Law to the word of the gospel (Rom 10:6–10). Like Moses, he accepts no excuse for Israel's failure to obey the good news made known to them (Rom 10:16–21).

30:14 in your mouth ... heart: The Law is made continuously present in Israel by frequent teaching and discussion of its commandments (6:6–7; 11:18–19).

30:15 life and good, death and evil: The two ways of the covenant. Choosing to love the Lord is the path to blessing (30:16), but turning away from him to serve idols leads to curses (30:17–18). The covenant options are likewise expressed in 11:26–28 and 28:1–68 (CCC 1696). • Everything good and evil is contained in these two ways: heaven and hell, Christ and the devil, height and depth. By grace, power is given to us from God to choose whatever we wish (St. Caesarius of Arles, *Sermons* 149, 1).

30:19 witness: Treaty documents of the ancient Near East invoked the gods as witnesses to the alliance. Deuteronomy follows this convention but, because God is a partner in the

covenant and not simply a third-party witness, the creation is summoned to witness the covenant instead (4:26; 31:28). Other witnesses mentioned in the book include the Song of Moses (31:19, 21) and the written text of Deuteronomy (31:26). See introduction: *Structure*.

31:1–23 Leadership over Israel is transferred from Moses to Joshua, who is *publicly* commissioned by Moses in front of the people (31:7–8) and *privately* commissioned by the Lord in the sanctuary (31:14–23). This transfer of authority takes place as the death of Moses draws near and Israel makes ready to enter the Promised Land. Because times of transition can be times of uncertainty and fear, words of reassurance punctuate the speeches (to the people, 31:6; to Joshua, 31:7–8, 23). For the suitability of Joshua to assume this role, see note on Num 27:18. • *Allegorically*, the death of Moses foreshadows the end of the Law, when its altar is left desolate and its sacrifices, priests, and ceremonies pass away. The succession of Moses by Joshua announces the coming of Jesus, when nations embrace the faith, churches are raised, altars are consecrated by the precious Blood of Christ, and priests minister the Word of God (Origen of Alexandria, *Homilies on Joshua* 2, 1).

31:2 a hundred and twenty: For the significance of this age, see note on 34:7. **go out and come in:** Moses is not to continue active military leadership over Israel (Num 27:17; Josh 14:11).

31:4 Sihon and Og: Kings of the Transjordan defeated under the command of Moses (Num 21:21–35; Josh 12:1–6).

ᶜGk: Heb lacks *If you obey the commandments of the* Lord *your God.*

Rereading of the Law Commanded

9 And Moses wrote this law, and gave it to the priests the sons of Levi, who carried the ark of the covenant of the Lord, and to all the elders of Israel. ¹⁰And Moses commanded them, "At the end of every seven years, at the set time of the year of release, at the feast of booths, ¹¹when all Israel comes to appear before the Lord your God at the place which he will choose, you shall read this law before all Israel in their hearing. ¹²Assemble the people, men, women, and little ones, and the sojourner within your towns, that they may hear and learn to fear the Lord your God, and be careful to do all the words of this law, ¹³and that their children, who have not known it, may hear and learn to fear the Lord your God, as long as you live in the land which you are going over the Jordan to possess."

Moses and Joshua Receive God's Charge

14 And the Lord said to Moses, "Behold, the days approach when you must die; call Joshua, and present yourselves in the tent of meeting, that I may commission him." And Moses and Joshua went and presented themselves in the tent of meeting. ¹⁵And the Lord appeared in the tent in a pillar of cloud; and the pillar of cloud stood by the door of the tent.

16 And the Lord said to Moses, "Behold, you are about to sleep with your fathers; then this people will rise and play the harlot after the strange gods of the land, where they go to be among them, and they will forsake me and break my covenant which I have made with them. ¹⁷Then my anger will be kindled against them in that day, and I will forsake them and hide my face from them, and they will be devoured; and many evils and troubles will come upon them, so that they will say in that day, 'Have not these evils come upon us because our God is not among us?' ¹⁸And I will surely hide my face in that day on account of all the evil which they have done,

because they have turned to other gods. ¹⁹Now therefore write this song, and teach it to the sons of Israel; put it in their mouths, that this song may be a witness for me against the sons of Israel. ²⁰For when I have brought them into the land flowing with milk and honey, which I swore to give to their fathers, and they have eaten and are full and grown fat, they will turn to other gods and serve them, and despise me and break my covenant. ²¹And when many evils and troubles have come upon them, this song shall confront them as a witness (for it will live unforgotten in the mouths of their descendants); for I know the purposes which they are already forming, before I have brought them into the land that I swore to give." ²²So Moses wrote this song the same day, and taught it to the sons of Israel.

23 And the Lord commissioned Joshua the son of Nun and said, "Be strong and of good courage; for you shall bring the children of Israel into the land which I swore to give them: I will be with you."

24 When Moses had finished writing the words of this law in a book, to the very end, ²⁵Moses commanded the Levites who carried the ark of the covenant of the Lord, ²⁶"Take this book of the law, and put it by the side of the ark of the covenant of the Lord your God, that it may be there for a witness against you. ²⁷For I know how rebellious and stubborn you are; behold, while I am yet alive with you, today you have been rebellious against the Lord; how much more after my death! ²⁸Assemble to me all the elders of your tribes, and your officers, that I may speak these words in their ears and call heaven and earth to witness against them. ²⁹For I know that after my death you will surely act corruptly, and turn aside from the way which I have commanded you; and in the days to come evil will befall you, because you will do what is evil in the sight of the Lord, provoking him to anger through the work of your hands."

31:9 Moses wrote: A claim that Moses is the author of the laws written in Deuteronomy (31:24). Mosaic authorship is also claimed for other parts of the Pentateuch, such as the record of Israel's battle with the Amalekites (Ex 17:14), the Decalogue and the Covenant Code (Ex 24:4, referring to Ex 20–23), the laws of the covenant renewal at Sinai (Ex 34:27, referring to Ex 34:11–26), the wilderness travelogue (Num 33:2, referring to Num 33:3–49), and the lyrics of the Song of Moses (31:19, referring to 32:1–43) (CCC 2056). • The belief that Moses wrote the books of the Torah is the universal ancient Jewish tradition. Witnesses to this belief in NT times include Jesus (Jn 5:46–47), the Sadducees (Mk 12:19), and Paul (Rom 10:5). **the priests:** The teachers and catechists of ancient Israel (33:10; Lev 10:11).

31:10 the year of release: Every seventh year when all debts are cancelled (15:1–3). **the feast of booths:** A seven-day pilgrim festival celebrated in the seventh liturgical month (16:13–15). See note on Lev 23:34–43.

31:11 the place: The location of Israel's century sanctuary (12:5). **read this law:** A reading of Deuteronomy before the assembled tribes of Israel. Ancient Near Eastern treaties also

set times for a public recitation of the stipulations to the treaty partners. See introduction: *Structure.*

31:14 the tent of meeting: The Mosaic Tabernacle.

31:16 play the harlot: An idiom for idolatry, a form of spiritual prostitution that degrades and defiles God's people (Ex 34:15; Num 25:1–2).

31:19 this song: Refers to the Song of Moses in 32:1–43, as do the other "song" references in 31:21–22.

31:24 in a book: I.e., in a written document rolled up as a scroll. For more on Moses as a writer, see note on 31:9.

31:26 the side of the ark: The Deuteronomy scroll is kept *beside* the Ark of the Covenant in the innermost room of the Tabernacle. This makes its precepts accessible to the priests, unlike the tablets of the Decalogue, which were kept *inside* the Ark of the Covenant (Ex 25:16; 40:20). For other differences between the covenant of Deuteronomy and the covenant at Sinai, see notes on 27:1–26 and 29:1.

31:28 heaven and earth: Witnesses to the covenant. See note on 30:19.

31:29 act corruptly: As the people did by worshiping the golden calf (9:12; Ex 32:7–8). **work of your hands:** A reference to man-made idols (4:28; 27:15).

The Song of Moses

30 Then Moses spoke the words of this song until they were finished, in the ears of all the assembly of Israel:

32 "Give ear, O heavens, and I will speak;
    and let the earth hear the words of my
        mouth.
²May my teaching drop as the rain,
    my speech distil as the dew,
as the gentle rain upon the tender grass,
    and as the showers upon the herb.
³For I will proclaim the name of the Lord.
    Ascribe greatness to our God!

⁴"The Rock, his work is perfect;
    for all his ways are justice.
A God of faithfulness and without iniquity,
    just and right is he.
⁵They have dealt corruptly with him,
    they are no longer his children because of their
        blemish;
    they are a perverse and crooked generation.
⁶Do you thus repay the Lord,
    you foolish and senseless people?
Is not he your father, who created you,
    who made you and established you?

⁷Remember the days of old,
    consider the years of many generations;
ask your father, and he will show you;
    your elders, and they will tell you.
⁸When the Most High gave to the nations their
        inheritance,
    when he separated the sons of men,
he fixed the bounds of the peoples
    according to the number of the sons of Israel.ᵈ
⁹For the Lord's portion is his people,
    Jacob his allotted heritage.

¹⁰"He found him in a desert land,
    and in the howling waste of the wilderness;
he encircled him, he cared for him,
    he kept him as the apple of his eye.
¹¹Like an eagle that stirs up its nest,
    that flutters over its young,
spreading out its wings, catching them,
    bearing them on its pinions,
¹²the Lord alone did lead him,
    and there was no foreign god with him.
¹³He made him ride on the high places of the earth,
    and he ate the produce of the field;
and he made him suck honey out of the rock,
    and oil out of the flinty rock.

32:5: Phil 2:15.

32:1–43 The Song of Moses. Its lyrics constitute a prophetic lawsuit against Israel for future violation of the Deuteronomic covenant. It *vindicates* the Lord as faithful (32:4), caring (32:10), and providing (32:13–14), while it *prosecutes* Israel for corruption (32:5), idolatry (32:15–16), and faithlessness (32:20). Combining elements of flashback and forecast, it looks back on the patriarchal period (32:7–9) and the wilderness wanderings (32:10–12), just as it also looks ahead to Israel's wayward life in Canaan (32:13–22), the judgments destined to follow (32:22–33), the return of God's mercy (32:36, 39), and the vengeance taken on the enemies of God's people (32:35, 40–43). The same story of rebellion and future restoration is outlined in the prose account of 30:1–10, although the Song frames it in terms of God's divine Fatherhood and Israel's divine sonship. • The NT references the Song of Moses several times. Jesus excerpts from it in Mt 17:17 and Lk 9:41 (32:5, 20); Peter alludes to it in Acts 2:40 (32:5); Paul refers to it in Acts 17:26 (32:8), Rom 10:19 (32:21), Rom 12:19 (32:35, resembles the Aramaic version), Rom 15:10 (32:43, the Greek version), 1 Cor 10:20, 22 (32:16–17, 21), and Phil 2:15 (32:5); the Book of Hebrews cites it in Heb 1:6 (32:43, Greek LXX version) and Heb 10:30 (32:35, resembles an Aramaic version); and the Book of Revelation quotes a line in Rev 19:2 (32:43).
    32:1 O heavens ... earth: The witnesses of the Deuteronomic covenant (4:26; 30:19; 31:28).
    32:4 The Rock: An epithet for the Lord throughout the Song (32:15, 18, 30–31), portraying him as the solid and secure foundation of Israel's life (Gen 49:24).
    32:5 dealt corruptly: Like the apostates of Israel who worshiped the golden calf at Mt. Sinai. The same expression is used in 9:12 and Ex 32:7–8. **his children:** Literally "his sons". The Song stresses the familial bond between the divine Father

(32:6) and his children (32:19–20). Kinship bonds are rooted in the covenant. See note on 1:31. **crooked generation:** Like the evil Exodus generation that came forth from Egypt but refused to enter Canaan (1:35).
    32:8 nations: Alludes to the Table of Nations in Gen 10:1–32, where 70 peoples descended from Noah's three sons repopulate the earth after the flood. These nations spread across the Near East (Shem), north Africa (Ham), and the northern Mediterranean into Europe (Japheth). Fixing the **bounds** of the nations suggests that God gave them specific land allotments with defined borders (CCC 57). **sons of Israel:** A translation of the Hebrew Masoretic text, which refers to the 70 members of Jacob's family who migrated to Egypt (Gen 46:27) and whose number corresponds to the 70 nations that appeared after the flood (Gen 10:1–32). A Hebrew fragment found among the Dead Sea Scrolls, along with some Greek manuscripts, read instead "the sons of God", which probably refers to the angels (Job 1:6; Ps 29:1). This alternative wording implies that God assigned patron angels to each of the world's nations (e.g., the angelic "princes" in Dan 10:13, 20; 12:1).
    32:10 apple: The small opening or pupil of the eye that is carefully guarded from harm (Ps 17:8).
    32:11 its young: Israel is compared to a baby eagle learning to fly under the watchful care of the Lord. For the image of God as a bird with protective wings, see also Is 31:5.
    32:13 the earth: Or "the land", suggesting a reference to Israel's upcoming settlement in Canaan, where the people first ate the harvest of the field since coming forth from Egypt (Josh 5:12). **honey ... rock:** Beehives in Canaan could be found in rock crevices (Is 7:18–19). Honey was one of the delicacies of the land (Ex 3:8; Ps 81:16). **oil ... rock:** Olive trees grow on the rocky terrain of Canaan. • *Allegorically*, the rock is Christ, and disciples draw honey from the rock when they see the sweetness of his miracles and draw oil from the rock when they receive the holy anointing of the Spirit (St. Gregory the Great, *Homilies on the Gospels* 26).

ᵈ Or *God*.

¹⁴Curds from the herd, and milk from the flock,
  with fat of lambs and rams,
    herds of Bashan and goats,
  with the finest of the wheat—
    and of the blood of the grape you drank wine.

¹⁵"But Jesh'urun waxed fat, and kicked;
  you waxed fat, you grew thick, you became
    sleek;
  then he forsook God who made him,
    and scoffed at the Rock of his salvation.
¹⁶They stirred him to jealousy with strange gods;
  with abominable practices they provoked him
    to anger.
¹⁷They sacrificed to demons which were no gods,
  to gods they had never known,
  to new gods that had come in of late,
    whom your fathers had never dreaded.
¹⁸You were unmindful of the Rock that begot ᵉ
    you,
  and you forgot the God who gave you birth.

¹⁹"The Lord saw it, and spurned them,
  because of the provocation of his sons and his
    daughters.
²⁰And he said, 'I will hide my face from them,
  I will see what their end will be,
  for they are a perverse generation,
    children in whom is no faithfulness.
²¹They have stirred me to jealousy with what is no
    god;
  they have provoked me with their idols.
So I will stir them to jealousy with those who are
    no people;
  I will provoke them with a foolish nation.

²²For a fire is kindled by my anger,
  and it burns to the depths of Sheol,
  devours the earth and its increase,
    and sets on fire the foundations of the
      mountains.

²³"'And I will heap evils upon them;
  I will spend my arrows upon them;
²⁴they shall be wasted with hunger,
  and devoured with burning heat
    and poisonous pestilence;
and I will send the teeth of beasts against
    them,
  with venom of crawling things of the dust.
²⁵In the open the sword shall bereave,
  and in the chambers shall be terror,
  destroying both young man and virgin,
    the sucking child with the man of gray
      hairs.
²⁶I would have said, "I will scatter them afar,
  I will make the remembrance of them cease
    from among men,"
²⁷had I not feared provocation by the enemy,
  lest their adversaries should judge amiss,
  lest they should say, "Our hand is triumphant,
    the Lord has not wrought all this."'

²⁸"For they are a nation void of counsel,
  and there is no understanding in them.
²⁹If they were wise, they would understand this,
  they would discern their latter end!
³⁰How should one chase a thousand,
  and two put ten thousand to flight,
  unless their Rock had sold them,
    and the Lord had given them up?

32:17: 1 Cor 10:20. 32:21: Rom 10:19; 11:11; 1 Cor 10:22.

32:14 Bashan: Lush pasturelands east of the Sea of Galilee. The region was notorious for its robust livestock (Ps 22:12; Ezek 39:18).

32:15 Jeshurun: An epithet for Israel in Deuteronomy (33:5, 26) and Isaiah (Is 44:2). Its meaning is debated. Some connect it with the Hebrew verb "to be upright" (*yashar*); others favor a wordplay on the Hebrew noun for "bull" (*shor*). The Greek LXX takes it to mean "the Beloved". waxed fat: Moses foresees Israel fattening itself on the luxuries of Canaan (31:20). • Once the Israelites enjoyed relief and freedom from bondage, they should have been more thankful and more eager to praise the Lord. But they did just the opposite and were ruined by their abundance of ease (St. John Chrysostom, *Baptismal Instructions* 5, 16).

32:16 jealousy: Triggered by idolatry. This forecast of the future evokes memories of Israel's idolatrous past—worship of the golden calf (Ex 32:1–6), sacrifices made to goat idols (Lev 17:7), and participation in the Baal cult of Peor (Num 25:1–3).

32:17 to demons: Sacrifice to idols is viewed as sacrifice to fallen spirits. Demons are not gods in the strict sense (32:21, 39) but are powerful spiritual beings that exert an evil influence upon their devotees. For this interpretation elsewhere in Scripture, see also Ps 106:37; Bar 4:7; 1 Cor 10:20.

32:18 gave you birth: The Lord is sometimes compared to a mother who gave birth to Israel (Is 49:15; CCC 239).

32:21 stir them to jealousy: Fitting discipline for provoking the Lord to jealous anger with idols. no people: Gentiles, who have no covenant relationship with God. The Lord will make Israel jealous when he includes Gentiles as members of his people. • According to Paul, this is fulfilled in messianic times when God accepts Gentiles into the Church in order to provoke Israel to a jealous imitation of their faith (Rom 10:19; 11:13–14). The discipline envisioned by the Song will thus have a saving effect upon Israel (Rom 11:25–26). See also note on 32:43.

32:22 Sheol: The realm of the dead. See word study: *Sheol* at Num 16:30.

32:23–25 Foresees covenant curses unleashed upon Israel in the future (listed in 28:15–68).

32:27 lest they should say: The annihilation of Israel would lead to misunderstanding and pride among its conquerors. In view of this, the Lord resolves to scatter his people (32:26), but not beyond remembrance or recall (30:3). The time will come when he pours out his mercy upon a surviving remnant (32:36).

32:28–33 The subject of these lines is debated. Some think Israel is the nation that lacks wisdom, but the enemy nation that God uses to punish his people is more likely intended.

ᵉ Or *bore*.

³¹For their rock is not as our Rock,
    even our enemies themselves being judges.
³²For their vine comes from the vine of Sodom,
    and from the fields of Gomor′rah;
  their grapes are grapes of poison,
    their clusters are bitter;
³³their wine is the poison of serpents,
    and the cruel venom of asps.

³⁴"Is not this laid up in store with me,
    sealed up in my treasuries?
³⁵Vengeance is mine, and recompense,
    for the time when their foot shall slip;
  for the day of their calamity is at hand,
    and their doom comes swiftly.
³⁶For the Lᴏʀᴅ will vindicate his people
    and have compassion on his servants,
  when he sees that their power is gone,
    and there is none remaining, bond or free.
³⁷Then he will say, 'Where are their gods,
    the rock in which they took refuge,
³⁸who ate the fat of their sacrifices,
    and drank the wine of their drink offering?
  Let them rise up and help you,
    let them be your protection!

³⁹" 'See now that I, even I, am he,
    and there is no god beside me;
  I kill and I make alive;
    I wound and I heal;
  and there is none that can deliver out of my
      hand.
⁴⁰For I lift up my hand to heaven,
    and swear, As I live for ever,

⁴¹if I sharpen my glittering sword,ᶠ
    and my hand takes hold on judgment,
  I will take vengeance on my adversaries,
    and will repay those who hate me.
⁴²I will make my arrows drunk with blood,
    and my sword shall devour flesh—
  with the blood of the slain and the captives,
    from the long-haired heads of the enemy.'

⁴³"Praise his people, O you nations;
    for he avenges the blood of his servants,
  and takes vengeance on his adversaries,
    and makes expiation for the land of his
      people."ᵍ

44 Moses came and recited all the words of this song in the hearing of the people, he and Joshuaʰ the son of Nun. ⁴⁵And when Moses had finished speaking all these words to all Israel, ⁴⁶he said to them, "Lay to heart all the words which I enjoin upon you this day, that you may command them to your children, that they may be careful to do all the words of this law. ⁴⁷For it is no trifle for you, but it is your life, and thereby you shall live long in the land which you are going over the Jordan to possess."

Moses' Death Foretold

48 And the Lᴏʀᴅ said to Moses that very day, ⁴⁹"Ascend this mountain of the Ab′arim, Mount Nebo, which is in the land of Moab, opposite Jericho; and view the land of Canaan, which I give to the sons of Israel for a possession; ⁵⁰and die on the mountain which you ascend, and be gathered to your people, as Aaron your brother died in Mount Hor and was gathered to his people; ⁵¹because you broke faith with me in the midst of the sons of Israel at

---

32:35: Rom 12:19; Heb 10:30. 32:43: Rom 15:10; Heb 1:6 (Septuagint); Rev 6:10; 19:2.

32:31 their rock: The patron god of the nation that overthrows Israel. Foreign deities such as this will afford their people no protection against the Lord's wrath (32:37–38).

32:35 Vengeance: The fearsome retribution of the Lord on the conquerors of Israel (32:41–43). The lesson is that justice and punishment belong to God rather than his people (Rom 12:19; Heb 10:30).

32:36 compassion: Mercy is the hope of Israel's future, as detailed in 30:3–10.

32:39 no god beside me: Restates the doctrine of monotheism set forth in earlier chapters (4:35, 39; 6:4). **I make alive:** The Lord has absolute authority over life and death (1 Sam 2:6; Tob 13:2). This is the foundation of the OT doctrine of the resurrection (Is 26:19; Dan 12:2; Hos 6:2). • It is certain that God causes death. It is also certain and worthy of faith that he makes alive. Believe this, that on the day of resurrection, your body will rise, and you will receive the reward of your faith from the Lord (St. Aphrahat, *Demonstrations* 9, 25).

32:40 lift up my hand: A ritual oath gesture (Rev 10:5–6). The Lord himself swears an oath to avenge his people with the sword of his judgment (32:41–42). **As I live:** The same formula is used in the divine oath of disinheritance in Num 14:21–25.

The idea is that God, the Supreme Being, cannot swear in the name of anything greater than himself, so when he takes an oath, he can only swear by his own life and name (Heb 6:13–18). See also Gen 22:16 and Ps 89:35.

32:43 Praise: This verse reads differently in the Greek LXX: "Rejoice, O heavens, with him, and let all the sons of God worship him. Rejoice, O nations, with his people, and let all the angels of God find strength in him. For he will avenge the blood of his sons, and he will exact vengeance and repay justice to his enemies. He will pay back those who hate him, and the Lord will cleanse his people's land." • Paul cites this LXX passage as confirmation that Israel and the Gentiles will worship side-by-side in the New Covenant (Rom 15:10). The Book of Hebrews excerpts from it to depict the angels worshiping the divine Lord (Heb 1:6). The Book of Revelation also cites a line from this verse, although it is closer to the Hebrew version than the Greek (Rev 19:2).

32:44 Joshua: The Hebrew reads "Hoshea", which is Joshua's birth name (see textual note h). See note on Num 13:8.

32:48 the Abarim: A highland range northeast of the Dead Sea. One of its mountains is Nebo, which rises over 2,600 feet and is called Pisgah (or, possibly, Pisgah is the mountain slope and Nebo is the summit). Peering out from this height, Moses had a panoramic view of Canaan before his death.

32:50 brother died: Aaron died earlier the same year, the fortieth year of the Exodus (compare 1:3 with Num 33:38). For the narrative account, see Num 20:22–29.

ᶠHeb *the lightning of my sword.*
ᵍGk Vg: Heb *his land his people.*
ʰGk Syr Vg: Heb *Hoshea.*

the waters of Mer'ibath-ka'desh, in the wilderness of Zin; because you did not revere me as holy in the midst of the sons of Israel. [52]For you shall see the land before you; but you shall not go there, into the land which I give to the sons of Israel."

Moses' Final Blessing

33 This is the blessing with which Moses the man of God blessed the children of Israel before his death. [2]He said,

"The LORD came from Sinai,
  and dawned from Se'ir upon us;[i]
  he shone forth from Mount Par'an,
he came from the ten thousands of holy ones,
  with flaming fire[j] at his right hand.
[3]Yes, he loved his people;[k]
  all those consecrated to him were in his[×]
    hand;
  so they followed[j] in your steps,
    receiving direction from you,
[4]when Moses commanded us a law,
  as a possession for the assembly of Jacob.
[5]Thus the LORD became king in Jesh'urun,
  when the heads of the people were gathered,
  all the tribes of Israel together.

[6]"Let Reuben live, and not die,
  nor let his men be few."

[7]And this he said of Judah:
"Hear, O LORD, the voice of Judah,
  and bring him in to his people.
With your hands contend[l] for him,
  and be a help against his adversaries."

[8]And of Levi he said,
"Give to Levi[m] your Thummim,
  and your U'rim to your godly one,
whom you tested at Massah,
  with whom you strove at the waters of
    Mer'ibah;
[9]who said of his father and mother,
  'I regard them not';
he disowned his brothers,
  and ignored his children.
For they observed your word,
  and kept your covenant.
[10]They shall teach Jacob your ordinances,
  and Israel your law;
they shall put incense before you,
  and whole burnt offering upon your altar.
[11]Bless, O LORD, his substance,
  and accept the work of his hands;
crush the loins of his adversaries,
  of those that hate him, that they rise not
    again."

[12]Of Benjamin he said,
"The beloved of the LORD,
  he dwells in safety by him;
he encompasses him all the day long,
  and makes his dwelling between his
    shoulders."

[13]And of Joseph he said,
"Blessed by the LORD be his land,
  with the choicest gifts of heaven above,[n]
  and of the deep that lies beneath,

32:52 not go there: Moses disqualified himself for entry into Canaan in Num 20:10–13. The event is recalled several times in Deuteronomy (1:37; 3:23–27; 4:21–22).

33:1–29 Moses invokes blessings on Israel's future life in Canaan. His words combine poetry and prayer like the patriarchal blessings in Genesis. Use of this model hints that Moses, like Isaac and Jacob before him, is cast in the role of a soon-to-die father (Gen 27:27–29; 49:1–27). The tribe of Simeon is omitted from the list of blessings, perhaps because this small tribe would eventually be assimilated into Judah. For the territories occupied by the twelve tribes, see Josh 13–19.

33:2–5 The Lord is a majestic Warrior, marching through the wilderness with Israel and an army of angels at his command. For similar depictions of this, see also Judg 5:4–5; Ps 68:7–18; Hab 3:3–15.

33:2 flaming fire: The Greek LXX reads "angels". Connecting this with 33:4, the belief arose that angels delivered the Mosaic Law to Israel. This is noted in Jewish writings (Josephus, *Antiquities* 15, 136) as well as the NT (Acts 7:53; Gal 3:19; Heb 2:2).

33:5 king: The kingship of the Lord is also noted in the Pentateuch in Ex 15:18 and Num 23:21. **Jeshurun:** A title for Israel. See note on 32:15.

33:6 nor let: Or "but let", expressing what follows in a negative rather than a positive way.

33:8 Thummim ... Urim: Sacred lots used to determine the Lord's will (Num 27:21). These small items, kept in the custody of the high priest (Ex 28:30), represent the priestly dignity conferred upon the Levitical family of Aaron (Ex 40:12–15).

33:9 disowned his brothers: Alludes to the golden calf apostasy, when the tribe of Levi heeded the call to slaughter fellow Israelites reveling in sin (Ex 32:25–29).

33:10 your law ... your altar: The Levites are ministers of word and sacrament in Israel, for the priests of the line of Aaron are charged with teaching the Law to the laity (24:8; Lev 10:11) and offering sacrifice and incense on their behalf (Lev 1:3–9; Num 16:40). No reference is made to Levi's territory, since this tribe did not receive a land inheritance in Canaan (18:1–2).

33:12 between his shoulders: In the lap or bosom of the Lord.

33:13 Joseph: Two tribes are blessed under this name, Ephraim and Manasseh (33:17), the two sons of Joseph, whom Jacob blessed and adopted as his own (Gen 48:1–22). There are several similarities between this blessing (33:13–17) and the blessing pronounced over the Joseph tribes by Jacob (Gen 49:22–26).

---

[i] Gk Syr Vg: Heb *them.*
[j] The meaning of the Hebrew word is uncertain.
[k] Gk: Heb *peoples.*
[×] Heb *your.*
[l] Cn: Heb *with his hands he contended.*
[m] Gk: Heb lacks *Give to Levi.*
[n] Two Heb Mss and Tg: Heb *with the dew.*

¹⁴with the choicest fruits of the sun,
    and the rich yield of the months,
¹⁵with the finest produce of the ancient mountains,
    and the abundance of the everlasting hills,
¹⁶with the best gifts of the earth and its fulness,
    and the favor of him that dwelt in the bush.
Let these come upon the head of Joseph,
    and upon the crown of the head of him that is
        prince among his brothers.
¹⁷His firstling bull has majesty,
    and his horns are the horns of a wild ox;
with them he shall push the peoples,
    all of them, to the ends of the earth;
such are the ten thousands of E'phraim,
    and such are the thousands of Manas'seh."

¹⁸And of Zeb'ulun he said,
"Rejoice, Zebulun, in your going out;
    and Is'sachar, in your tents.
¹⁹They shall call peoples to their mountain;
    there they offer right sacrifices;
for they suck the affluence of the seas
    and the hidden treasures of the sand."

²⁰And of Gad he said,
"Blessed be he who enlarges Gad!
    Gad lurks like a lion,
he tears the arm, and the crown of the head.
²¹He chose the best of the land for himself,
    for there a commander's portion was
        reserved;
and he came to the heads of the people,
    with Israel he executed the commands
    and just decrees of the Lord."

²²And of Dan he said,
"Dan is a lion's whelp,
    that leaps forth from Bashan."

²³And of Naph'tali he said,
"O Naphtali, satisfied with favor,
    and full of the blessing of the Lord,
        possess the lake and the south."

²⁴And of Asher he said,
"Blessed above sons be Asher;
    let him be the favorite of his brothers,
    and let him dip his foot in oil.
²⁵Your bars shall be iron and bronze;
    and as your days, so shall your strength be.

²⁶"There is none like God, O Jesh'urun,
    who rides through the heavens to your help,
    and in his majesty through the skies.
²⁷The eternal God is your dwelling place,
    and underneath are the everlasting arms.
And he thrust out the enemy before you,
    and said, Destroy.
²⁸So Israel dwelt in safety,
    the fountain of Jacob alone,
in a land of grain and wine;
    yes, his heavens drop down dew.
²⁹Happy are you, O Israel! Who is like you,
    a people saved by the Lord,
the shield of your help,
    and the sword of your triumph!
Your enemies shall come fawning to you;
    and you shall tread upon their high places."

The Death of Moses

34 And Moses went up from the plains of Moab to Mount Nebo, to the top of Pisgah, which is opposite Jericho. And the Lord showed him all the land, Gilead as far as Dan, ²all Naph'tali, the land of E'phraim and Manas'seh, all the land of Judah as far as the western sea, ³the Neg'eb, and the Plain, that is, the valley of Jericho the city of palm trees, as far as Zoar. ⁴And the Lord said to him, "This is the land

---

33:16 the bush: The burning bush at Sinai (Ex 3:1–3).

33:17 firstling: Perhaps an allusion to the first-born birthright that was taken away from Jacob's oldest son, Reuben (Gen 49:3–4), and given to the younger Joseph (1 Chron 5:1–2).

33:19 their mountain: Either Mt. Carmel on the Mediterranean coast or Mt. Tabor in lower Galilee (Judg 4:6). **affluence of the seas:** Prosperity gained from maritime trade. **treasures of the sand:** Perhaps a reference to seashells (from the murex snail) known to yield an expensive purple dye.

33:21 best of the land: Gad made a bid for the choice grazing lands east of the Jordan (Num 32:1–5).

33:22 Bashan: The fertile region east of the Sea of Galilee. Its pasturelands supported abundant livestock, and its forestlands gave cover to carnivorous predators such as lions. Some read this passage as an allusion to the Danite migration into northern Israel near Bashan, but this is not demanded by the text (Josh 19:47; Judg 18).

33:23 the lake: The Sea of Galilee.

33:24 oil: From the olive orchards that flourished in the northern territory of Asher.

33:26–29 The final blessing is for the whole family of Israel, that the Lord will give his tribes victory and establish them in the Promised Land.

33:26 rides through the heavens: Evokes the image of the Lord riding the clouds as his battle chariot (Ps 104:3; Is 19:1).

33:27 dwelling place: Or "refuge".

33:29 high places: Mountains and hilltops where Canaanite shrines were often built. Israel was ordered to demolish these cultic sites and obliterate idolatry from the land (7:5; 12:2–3).

34:1–12 Appears to be a later addition to the Book of Deuteronomy, whose laws are otherwise ascribed to Moses (31:9, 22, 24). Two considerations point in this direction. **(1)** The chapter serves as Moses' obituary, in which case someone other than Moses is likely to have written it. **(2)** The historical notations in 34:6 ("to this day") and 34:10 ("since") imply that the narrator was part of a later generation looking back on the life and legacy of Moses from a distance.

34:1 Mount Nebo: Rises east of the Jordan near its termination at the Dead Sea. See note on 32:48. **all the land:** The geography of 34:1–3 describes a visual sweep of Canaan from north to south.

34:2 the western sea: The Mediterranean Sea.

of which I swore to Abraham, to Isaac, and to Jacob, 'I will give it to your descendants.' I have let you see it with your eyes, but you shall not go over there." [5]So Moses the servant of the Lord died there in the land of Moab, according to the word of the Lord, [6]and he buried him in the valley in the land of Moab opposite Beth-pe′or; but no man knows the place of his burial to this day. [7]Moses was a hundred and twenty years old when he died; his eye was not dim, nor his natural force abated. [8]And the sons of Israel wept for Moses in the plains of Moab thirty days; then the days of weeping and mourning for Moses were ended.

[9] And Joshua the son of Nun was full of the spirit of wisdom, for Moses had laid his hands upon him; so the sons of Israel obeyed him, and did as the Lord had commanded Moses. [10]And there has not arisen a prophet since in Israel like Moses, whom the Lord knew face to face, [11]none like him for all the signs and the wonders which the Lord sent him to do in the land of Egypt, to Pharaoh and to all his servants and to all his land, [12]and for all the mighty power and all the great and terrible deeds which Moses wrought in the sight of all Israel.

34:10: Num 12:6–8.

34:6 he buried him: I.e., the Lord buried Moses in an unmarked grave in Moab. The Greek LXX reads "they buried him", implying that Israelites conducted the funeral rite. **Beth-peor:** A shrine to the Canaanite god, Baal. See note on 3:29.

34:7 a hundred and twenty: The maximum age limit for humanity established in Gen 6:3, which goes into full effect by the end of the Pentateuch. The lifetime of Moses can be divided into three equal periods of 40 years each (Acts 7:23, 30, 36). **Nor ... abated:** By an extraordinary grace, Moses appeared to be in the prime of life at the time of his death.

34:8 thirty days: A customary bereavement period after the death of a great leader (Num 20:29).

34:9 laid his hands: The imposition of hands signals an ordination to covenant leadership. Moses performed this rite upon Joshua in Num 27:18. See word study: *Lay* at Num 8:10.

34:10 face to face: Moses enjoyed an unparalleled intimacy with God in OT times (Num 12:6–8). Presumably none but the messianic "prophet like Moses" would be as close to the Lord as he. For more on this expected prophet, see note on 18:15.

34:11 signs ... wonders: Displays of divine might. The miracles of the Exodus are specifically in view (4:34; 6:22; Ex 7:3).

STUDY QUESTIONS
Deuteronomy

Chapter 1

For understanding
1. **1:3.** What is meant by the "fortieth year"? Though the trip should have lasted less than two years, what refusal of the Israelites caused it to take so long? When does the eleventh month fall?
2. **1:8.** To which land does Moses refer, and how far does it extend? When does Israel finally control the full extent of this territory? To what does "the LORD swore" refer?
3. **1:31.** How is the Lord portrayed here? What characteristics of God and the Israelites does the book highlight several times? In what is this type of kinship language rooted?
4. **1:39.** Whom does Moses call "your little ones"? Because persons younger than 20 years old were not eligible for military service, for what were they not held responsible? To what does "no knowledge of good and evil" refer?

For application
1. **1:6.** Think of a time when you felt you needed to make a major change in your life, even if your circumstances at the time were both good and comfortable. What inspired the urge to make the change? Were you aware then or later that the desire to change came from the Lord?
2. **1:13.** According to 1 Tim 3:2–7, what qualifications should one look for in a bishop? How many of these qualifications are still pertinent? What other qualifications in Church leaders may be necessary or desirable? How often do you pray for your bishop?
3. **1:26–28.** Have you ever been given a task or a project that you were afraid was too great for you? If so, what did you do to avoid it? If avoidance was not possible, what was your attitude as you began it?
4. **1:41–44.** If at first you refused the task you feared, what were the consequences? How did you try to recover from them? For example, if you changed your mind and tried to complete the task anyway, how successful were your efforts? What did you learn from the experience?

Chapter 2

For understanding
1. **2:1–3:11.** What do these verses describe? At this time, with whom do the Israelites avoid conflict, but against whom do they take up arms? With what historical notes is the account interspersed? In seizing Amorite lands by force of arms, among whom does Israel take its place?
2. **2:9.** Where was Moab, and what were its borders? From whom are both Moabites and Ammonites descended?
3. **2:14.** To what does the time lapse of thirty-eight years refer? Since that time, who perished, who survived, and what happened to the children of the first generation, the conquest generation? What oath had the Lord sworn to them?
4. **2:30.** How does the Lord bring judgment on Sihon? As one of the wicked idolaters, why must he be cleared away?

For application
1. **2:7.** In what spiritual wanderings have you engaged? Where have they led you? Given that the Lord knows what you have been through, how has he helped you get to where you are?
2. **2:14.** Assuming that a generation is roughly 40 years, which generation is passing from us, and which is coming into ascendancy? Which elements of our previous generation's religious heritage have been passed on, and which are being rejected or replaced?
3. **2:27–29.** Why do foreign countries require the presentation of a passport before you can enter their territory? What happens if you attempt to enter the country without one or if you lose it while there?
4. **2:30.** Why do you think that Sihon, who was ignorant of God's plan, refused to grant Israel's request to purchase provisions and pass through his country? Is hardness of heart the same as mere stubbornness? Though the text says that God hardened Sihon's spirit, who actually hardened it?

Chapter 3

For understanding
1. **3:11.** Who is Og? What is meant by "his bedstead"? How large was it, how was it built, and where was it on display for a time?
2. **3:18.** What does Moses require of the fighting men of Reuben, Gad, and Manasseh?
3. **3:25.** What is Moses' final plea? Though the request is denied, what small consolation is given to him?
4. **3:29.** What is Beth-peor? How does reference to this location help to establish the context for Deuteronomy as a whole? What opportunity does the covenant of Deuteronomy give Israel?

For application
1. **3:3–6.** Given the description of the cities in Og's kingdom, how difficult must it have been for Israel to conquer them? What very difficult project have you completed, and what pleasure have you had in the effort it took?
2. **3:11.** Why do you think Moses adds this detail? What overwhelming spiritual difficulties have you faced and overcome?
3. **3:18.** Read the note for this verse. Since the tribes of Reuben, Gad, and Manasseh now have their inheritance, what motivation do they have for supporting the remaining tribes in getting theirs? If you gain what you have earned with effort, why should you help others?

4. **3:23–26.** Have you ever sought permission from the Lord to accomplish a much-desired work? How did the Lord reveal his answer? If the answer was negative, how did you receive it?

Chapter 4

For understanding
1. **4:6.** How does the Torah benefit Israel as a guide to living for the glory of God? What effect will the moral and spiritual witness have on neighboring nations?
2. **4:12.** Why must the Lord not be depicted in the form of any created thing? What did the imageless worship required by the first commandment of the Decalogue act as a way of accomplishing? God, who is spirit, did not assume a physical form until what happened?
3. **4:24.** In what way does the Lord act as a devouring fire? How does he render this mystery concrete? According to Origen of Alexandria, what does the God of fire consume?
4. **4:35.** What does the expression of Israel's monotheistic faith affirm, and what does it deny? What does it claim? To what extent is the existence of "other gods" still acknowledged? If the basis for this claim is not philosophical reasoning, what is it?
5. **Word Study: Loved (4:37).** How is *'ahab*, the Hebrew verb "to love", used variously in the OT? As a key theme in Deuteronomy, what kind of love is it? In this respect, as in others, how does Deuteronomy parallel Near Eastern vassal treaties? What does a suzerain king swear to do, and what does the vassal swear to do? In Deuteronomy, what does the Lord as king do, and how are the Israelites commanded to love the Lord?

For application
1. **4:2.** Notice the wording of this verse. What does not adding to or subtracting from the Lord's word have to do with obedience to the commandments themselves? For example, how would adding or removing requirements to the Lord's word potentially corrupt it?
2. **4:5–6.** What is the evangelistic rationale for obeying the Ten Commandments? How does observance of the commandments demonstrate wisdom and understanding?
3. **4:24.** Note the context for this verse. If God is infinite, eternal, and omnipotent, what cause has he to be jealous? How jealous should God be for his people today?
4. **4:29.** As exiles on earth in a militantly secularist culture, how are we to seek the Lord our God? According to this verse, what is the condition for seeking him successfully?

Chapter 5

For understanding
1. **5:5.** When was Moses elected to the role of mediator of divine revelation to Israel? How were all laws given subsequent to the Decalogue relayed to the people?
2. **Essay: What Is a Covenant?** Why is the covenant motif in the Bible more pervasive and important than other covenants in the ancient Near East? As formal agreements between two parties that are sealed by oath, what do covenants accomplish, especially as a mutual exchange of persons? What formal procedures were necessary to ratify a covenant and make it binding? What three forms could covenants assume depending on their function? Though covenants in Scripture follow conventional models and procedures of the biblical world, how are they nevertheless unique?
3. **5:6–21.** Although the list of the Ten Commandments here and in Ex 20:1–17 are substantially the same, how are they different? Which order does traditional catechesis follow?
4. **5:22.** How did the Lord give the commandments? What is the twofold significance of the statement that the Lord "added no more"?

For application
1. **5:2.** Read the essay "What Is a Covenant?" How does the Mosaic covenant pertain to Christians today? How does the New Covenant in Jesus Christ incorporate the Old?
2. **5:3.** Why does Moses make this statement? How are you personally incorporated into the New Covenant?
3. **5:6–21.** Jews look upon these commandments not only as obligations but as opportunities to do good works. How does each commandment provide such opportunities for you?
4. **5:32.** How does this verse reflect Jesus' injunction to enter by the "narrow gate" (Mt 7:13–14)?

Chapter 6

For understanding
1. **6:4.** What does this solemn address, used several times in the book, introduce here? How often each day have devout Jews recited this prayer since ancient times? What does the confession of faith in the Lord's oneness and uniqueness affirm? While the NT affirms the oneness of God revealed in the OT, how does it expand this belief? According to St. Fulgentius, while we say that the Father, Son, and Spirit are one God in a unity of nature, what do we dare not say?
2. **6:7.** What kind of school is the family? Upon whom does responsibility for the spiritual formation of children rest?
3. **6:8–9.** What Jewish tradition did these verses inspire? What are phylacteries? What are mezuzot?
4. **6:16.** What mistake is this verse a warning not to repeat? When does Jesus defend himself with this verse?

For application
1. **6:5.** If love of God is considered not to be sentimental but an action, how do you love God with all your heart and soul? Assuming that strength includes all your resources, what does it mean to love him with all your strength?

2. **6:7.** How comprehensive of all your daily activity is Moses' injunction to teach your children? In *Catechesi Tradendae*, Pope John Paul II says that in catechesis Jesus is the one who is taught. How do you "teach Jesus" to your children?
3. **6:10-12.** Given all the good things Moses mentions, how could one forget the Lord? How have you shown gratitude for the good things you have? How often do you remember to thank him for them?
4. **6:20-25.** How does the explanation given by the father answer the question of his son as to the meaning of the commandments? For the Christian, how important is obedience to the commandments (cf. Jn 14:15)?

Chapter 7

For understanding
1. **7:1-5.** What must Israelites maintain? At what levels are associations with Canaanites forbidden?
2. **7:3.** Why does Deuteronomy forbid mixed marriages? To what will failure to heed this warning lead?
3. **7:6-8.** What theology does Moses expound? On what is the divine choice to set Israel apart as a holy nation based, and how is it expressed? In the economy of salvation, what greater end was the election of one nation as God's people a means to achieving?
4. **Word Study: Possession (7:6).** What does the Hebrew word *segullah* mean, often with what connotation? As a secular term, to what can it refer? As a theological term, what does it describe? Later in the OT, when a time of judgment becomes necessary, what does the Lord promise to do? How does the idea of a *segullah* carry over into the NT?
5. **7:22.** How is the conquest of Canaan, here described as a gradual process, elsewhere envisioned? How are both predictions true?

For application
1. **7:3-4.** Why do marriages between Catholics and baptized Christians of other denominations require permission from the bishop? Why do marriages between Christians and unbaptized persons require a dispensation? Why does Baptism make such a big difference?
2. **7:8.** Why has the Lord redeemed you? What return can you make to him for that grace?
3. **7:22.** How quickly have you rid yourself of all your sins and imperfections? Why is it a grace that you must conquer these things little by little? If you persevere, how certain is it that victory over them will be yours?
4. **7:26.** What occasions have the Internet and social media given you to bring an "abominable thing" such as pornography into your home, even if accidentally? What can be done to prevent this?

Chapter 8

For understanding
1. **8:3.** As the bread from heaven that sustained Israel during its long journey through the wilderness, what did the daily provision of manna express? What did the miracle of the manna teach Israel? What does ignorance of the word of God do to the human spirit? How does Jesus use this verse?
2. **8:5.** How does the Lord act as a man does who disciplines his son? Of what is discipline, though unpleasant, a sure sign? Among other things, what is it meant to induce? From what does the father-son relationship between the Lord and Israel arise?
3. **8:14.** To what does the concern about Israel's heart being lifted up refer? What is the danger?

For application
1. **8:2.** Psalm 139 ends with this invitation: "Search me, O God, and know my heart! Try me and know my thoughts" (Ps 139:23). How often have you issued to the Lord this invitation to test you? Why is it good for you that he puts you to the test from time to time?
2. **8:3.** How does the experience of hunger and its satisfaction with manna lead Israel to know that man lives only by what comes from the mouth of God? How does God create? How does the Eucharist, without which we have no life, come forth from the mouth of God?
3. **8:5.** A disciple can receive discipline in a variety of ways. How has the Lord disciplined you, either directly through prayer and spiritual exercises or indirectly through other life experiences? What are some positive and negative lessons you have learned from him?
4. **8:11-14.** How can a comfortable life pose a spiritual danger? If your Christian life is comfortable and serene, what can you do to avoid this danger?
5. **8:17.** Which commandment does the sin of presumption violate? What are the two kinds of presumption (CCC 2092)? How does presumption open the door to lax spiritual practice and carelessness of heart (CCC 2733)?

Chapter 9

For understanding
1. **9:4.** Why does the Lord plead for Israel's humility in view of its possession of the land of Canaan? On what is its possession based? According to St. John Cassian, morally, when we achieve success in warring against the vices of the flesh and have gained freedom from the world's way of life, why should we not be puffed up with the success?
2. **9:6—10:11.** What two critical events at the start of the wilderness period do these verses present?
3. **9:9.** After the covenant was first ratified at Sinai, what did Moses do? What happened when he finally came down?
4. **9:22-23.** With what are the sites mentioned in these verses associated? Besides the apostasy at Sinai, what did the people do at each one?

For application

1. **9:6.** How good do you have to be before you can merit God's grace? If your goodness does not prompt him to give you grace, what does?
2. **9:7, 24.** From where does the human urge to rebel against the Lord come? How deeply embedded in the heart is the spirit of rebellion? How can that spirit still be present even in the desire to submit to the Lord?
3. **9:18-19.** Do you ever practice intercessory prayer? What makes such prayer difficult? For whom do you intercede, and how long have you been doing it? Have you ever faced the temptation to give up?

Chapter 10

For understanding

1. **10:8.** What were the Levites tasked with doing in the wilderness? Which clan was responsible for carrying the ark? For what purpose was the Levitical family of Aaron ordained?
2. **10:16.** As an outward sign of an inward act, what does removing the foreskin of the flesh symbolize? What does it mean to have an uncircumcised heart?
3. **10:17.** What does the superlative expression "Lord of lords" mean? Given the covenant framework of Deuteronomy, what does it mean in particular? What does it mean to say that the Lord is not partial?
4. **10:18.** For whom does Deuteronomy express humanitarian concern? To what do its laws appeal?

For application

1. **10:5.** How do you store important personal papers such as contracts, property deeds, and certificates? How important are considerations such as their safety and access to them? What about the storage and care of sacred objects in your home?
2. **10:8.** From where does the right of the laity to administer blessings come? What are the limitations on this privilege (CCC 1669, 2626)?
3. **10:16.** As a metaphor for purification of intention, what are the limitations of the expression "circumcision of heart"? What metaphor would you use to get across the same idea?
4. **10:17.** Calling the Lord "the terrible God" can have several layers of meaning. What are some of them? In what sense might the negative connotations of the word be appropriate when applied to God, and how might they be inappropriate?

Chapter 11

For understanding

1. **11:6.** Who are Dathan and Abiram?
2. **11:10.** How were the farmlands of Egypt irrigated? Why will such toilsome labor not be necessary in Canaan?
3. **11:14.** In Palestine, when do the early and late rains come? When are crops sown, and how long does the harvest season stretch? According to St. Gregory the Great, what does rain represent allegorically, and when did the Lord give the early and the later rains?
4. **11:29-32.** What do these verses describe? On which twin mountains will it take place? While the liturgy is described in Deut 27:1-26, when will it be enacted?

For application

1. **11:8.** How does obedience to the commandments make one strong? In a culture like ours, what kinds of strength are needed?
2. **11:10.** What is the "land" that the Christian is called to go in and possess? How is it unlike the environment in which you live now?
3. **11:18, 20.** What ways do you have of reminding yourself of the word of God throughout your day? Do you carry anything with you or post anything in your house to help remind you? When you study Scripture, what means do you use to remember what you read?
4. **11:19.** Even if you send your children to religious education classes, what do you do to instruct your children directly and personally? How do you monitor what they are taught in these classes? How do you pray with them? How do you model your faith for them?

Chapter 12

For understanding

1. **12:1—26:19.** Just as chapters 5-11 outline the *general* stipulations of the covenant, what do these chapters set forth? In doing so, what pattern does Deuteronomy follow?
2. **12:5.** As the law of the central sanctuary, to what does it point? What is the twofold purpose of this law? What does centralizing worship at a single sanctuary thus foster? To what does selecting a single "place" for sacrifice stand in contrast? When does God reveal that Jerusalem is the chosen location? For what is "his name" an idiom, and what does it *not* mean that Deuteronomy is naïvely doing?
3. **12:13.** What legislation does this verse revise, and when will it go into effect? Centuries later, what does the prophet Malachi envision?
4. **12:15.** What did legislation in Leviticus stipulate about the profane slaughter of animals? Why is the Levitical law being revised now? In Deuteronomy, then, where may one slaughter animals, but for sacrifice where must they be slaughtered? Which animals may be slaughtered and eaten like game animals taken in hunting? What is the one exception?

For application

1. **12:2–3.** Why do we not follow the command in these verses today? How should Christians approach the idolatry rampant in our culture?
2. **12:5–7.** The note for verse 5 explains the rationale behind requiring Israel to worship through sacrifice in one place (later identified as Jerusalem). Where may Catholics conduct formal worship through the Eucharistic sacrifice? What is the rationale for that?
3. **12:23.** Both here and in Leviticus, the prohibition against consuming blood is stressed. How does that explain the defection of many of Jesus' disciples in Jn 6:66?
4. **12:30.** Why does Moses forbid curiosity over pagan worship practices? What would he have said about certain Eastern religious practices, such as transcendental meditation and yoga? How can curiosity about such things lead one into serious sin?

Chapter 13

For understanding

1. **13:1–18.** With what are these laws concerned? What must happen to instigators of idolatry? Likewise, what must happen to towns that forsake the Lord for other gods? Why is idolatry a capital offense?
2. **13:3.** According to St. Vincent of Lérins, as Deuteronomy indicates, why would divine Providence permit a teacher of the Church to wander from the faith? Who is the true and genuine Catholic?
3. **13:16.** How does the military operation have a cultic dimension? What must happen to the town that has been destroyed?
4. **13:17.** In this context, what are devoted things? Why must a complete ban be placed on all persons and property found in apostate cities?

For application

1. **13:1–5.** Jesus worked numerous miracles; why were they not enough to convince his critics to believe him? What impact might this regulation from Deuteronomy have had on how the Pharisees and Sadducees regarded Jesus?
2. **13:5.** Read the note for this verse. What are the penalties in the Church for teaching heresy? Why is the Church seemingly slow to impose them?
3. **13:17.** Look up 1 Sam 15:7–22. How completely did King Saul claim he fulfilled the command to impose the ban on the Amalekites? What did Samuel tell him he should have done? What was Saul's punishment? What happens to us if we do not banish sin from our lives?

Chapter 14

For understanding

1. **14:1.** In what is the adoptive sonship of Israel rooted? Why are self-laceration and shaving of the head forbidden?
2. **14:3.** For what are the ox, the sheep, and the goat worthy of use? Unlike Leviticus, why does Deuteronomy mention them specifically?
3. **14:21.** Why is it unlawful to boil a kid in its mother's milk?
4. **14:22–29.** What does the law of tithing require Israelite farmers to do with their annual harvest? Although part of the offering is eaten by the farmer and his family at the sanctuary, where does the rest go? Because the transportation of produce is difficult over long distances, what provision is made regarding food offerings? What happens with the tithe every third year?

For application

1. **14:3.** In the context of this chapter, how does the avoidance of certain foods contribute to the holiness of the people? According to Mark's Gospel, what reasoning did Jesus use to "declare all foods clean" (Mk 7:15–19)?
2. **14:21.** Why can an Israelite eat an animal that he slaughters but not one that dies naturally, although he is allowed to give or sell it to non-Israelites? What might this regulation have to do with the law against eating blood?
3. **14:22.** Do you practice tithing? If so, is it in the form of money? What other forms of income or personal resources might you tithe? How is almsgiving different from tithing?

Chapter 15

For understanding

1. **15:1.** As a new law added to the Sabbatical year of Exodus and Leviticus, what does Deuteronomy require in addition to letting fields lie fallow? What situation was periodic debt relief designed to balance? What was one problem that might result from this law?
2. **15:3.** Who does not qualify for the sabbatical release? What double standard does Deuteronomy thus erect for Israel and the people of other nations?
3. **15:12–18.** How does the law of slave release upgrade the law of Ex 21:1–11? Without provisions, what might happen to a newly released slave?
4. **15:16.** What does the refusal of a slave to be released indicate about domestic slavery? How was slavery beneficial in harsh economic conditions?

For application

1. **15:3.** The Catholic Church claims to exercise a "preferential option for the poor". What does that mean in practice? When it comes to choosing between helping Christian brethren and non-Christians, to whom do you owe priority of consideration?
2. **15:6.** Why is borrowing from a relative less problematic than borrowing from a stranger? On the other hand, what problems can arise from being in debt to a relative?

3. **15:11.** What questions about divine Providence do you have from the fact that poverty never seems to be eradicated? What social structures have been created to address this problem? Why do they always seem to fall short?
4. **15:12–18.** Suppose you wanted to employ a fellow Catholic who needed help supporting his family. What provisions for employment would you need to make for him? If, after a time, he felt able to support himself, what arrangements might you make for discharging him? How might the pattern of employment and discharge in these verses help you make the necessary decisions?

Chapter 16

For understanding
1. **16:1–17.** What does Deuteronomy do to Israel's three major feasts? As times of national assembly and worship, where are they to be celebrated?
2. **16:1.** What month of Israel's calendar is Abib, and what is it later called? When does it fall? What does Passover commemorate, and when is it celebrated?
3. **16:13.** When is the Feast of Booths celebrated, and what is it also called? What would take place for the pilgrims assembled for this feast every seventh year?
4. **16:18.** What role do judges and officers play? Although Deuteronomy does not specify who manned these local tribunals, who does it seem likely were represented? Where did the priestly tribe of Levi settle in Israel?

For application
1. **16:1–8.** How do you celebrate the Holy Week liturgies? When is the last time you attended a Chrism Mass with the bishop? What efforts do you make to participate in Good Friday and Easter Vigil services? If you do not participate in these, what prevents you?
2. **16:9–12.** What does the Feast of Pentecost mean to you? If you helped RCIA candidates to receive the Sacraments of Initiation at Easter, how do you conclude mystagogy at this feast? How does Pentecost prompt you to renew your own Confirmation?
3. **16:16–17.** Which liturgical feasts do you most enjoy? What is there about them that most delights you? How do you celebrate them? If they are also commercially popular, how do you retain their religious significance?

Chapter 17

For understanding
1. **17:6.** How were allegations verified for a death sentence to be issued in Israel? As further legal protection for the accused, with what does the Law threaten false witnesses?
2. **17:8–13.** What kinds of cases is a federal court established to handle? Where do members of this supreme tribunal convene? What kind of offense is failure to comply with its decisions?
3. **17:14–20.** What law is described here, and when does it go into effect? Why will the elevation of a human king be a divine concession to the weakness of Israel? What does Deuteronomy foresee among the dangers of adopting this model of government? What events will these types of selfish excess trigger?
4. **17:18.** In addition to the king's personal copy of Deuteronomy, what was to happen with the official scroll? Why must the king be an exemplary student of the Torah?

For application
1. **17:1.** When you come to the Lord in prayer, what do you offer him? In Rom 12:1–2, what sacrifice are you bringing to him? How do you make that sacrifice holy and pleasing to him?
2. **17:7.** Why does Moses lay on witnesses the responsibility of executing the death sentence? If you had been among the accusers of the woman caught in adultery (Jn 8:4–7), what would you have done when Jesus challenged you to cast the first stone? Why?
3. **17:12.** In a culture like ours, what is the responsibility of officers of the law when a judicial decision is rendered? What should happen to one who refuses to abide by the decision of the courts in the belief that the decision is unjust or immoral?
4. **17:18.** Some people think it is useful in Scripture study to write in a Bible; others disagree. What is your opinion? What is the benefit for yourself of writing notes (whether in the Bible or not)? What use do you make of memorization?

Chapter 18

For understanding
1. **18:1.** For what is "the Levitical priests" a general term? What clear distinction did legislation found in Exodus, Leviticus, and Numbers make between them? Why is Deuteronomy not concerned with this difference? As descendants of the patriarch Levi, the son of Jacob (Ex 6:16–25), in which family line do its priests stand? Because Levi is the one landless tribe in Israel, where will the Levites go to live?
2. **18:9–14.** What does Deuteronomy condemn in these verses? In the ancient Near East, what did occult practitioners often seek to learn about or influence? To this end, in what practices did they engage? Why is it significant that these laws immediately precede Moses' instruction regarding true prophecy in Israel?
3. **18:15.** Who will be the "prophet like me"? Since Moses himself is the model who defines the expectation, what does it suggest that the prophet to come will be like? What do many scholars think the passage envisions? That said, with whom did Jewish expectations during NT times identify the prophet like Moses? Where can this be seen? Regardless, then, of how this prediction might apply to various prophets in the OT, who fulfills the expectation of a prophet like Moses, and where is this first revealed?
4. **18:22.** How is a prophet proven to be false? How is he also exposed as a fraud?

For application
1. **18:2.** Moses reminds the Levites that they have no physical inheritance but that the Lord is their inheritance. What did that mean for their livelihood? What is the inheritance of men and women who take vows of perpetual poverty? What should happen for the support of aged religious who cannot support themselves?
2. **18:11-12.** What are some occult practices that exist in our culture? Why are these forbidden? Why is it dangerous to dabble in them, even as a parlor game?
3. **18:15.** The note for this verse refers to the Transfiguration (Mt 17:5), where the Father's words "listen to him" were directed to Peter, James, and John. Why especially to them? For you, what does it mean to "listen" to the prophet like Moses?
4. **18:21-22.** The charism of prophecy still exists and is exercised in various contexts in the Church. How do you discern whether a prophecy is true and reliable? Since post-biblical prophecy is private revelation, what attention should be paid to it?

Chapter 19

For understanding
1. **19:2.** What are the three cities for? Three asylum cities had already been assigned east of the Jordan; now where are three others assigned? How does Deuteronomy build on Num 35:9-34? Where are the cities of refuge listed by name?
2. **19:15-21.** What does the law of witnesses stipulate? How is legal protection for the innocent afforded in the law? What punishment do perjurers receive?
3. **19:21.** What standard does "eye for eye" provide? What compromises justice?

For application
1. **19:6.** In our system of justice, who takes on the role of the "avenger of blood"? Whether the crime is murder or manslaughter, what is the "avenger's" role when the culprit is caught? What is the role of relatives in our system of justice?
2. **19:12.** According to the revised version of CCC 2267, what does the Church say about recourse to the death penalty? If, despite past toleration of capital punishment, imposition of the death penalty is now "inadmissible", does that mean that it should never be imposed?
3. **19:18-19.** Why is perjury such a pernicious crime? What is the penalty for perjury in our society?
4. **19:21.** In the context of this passage, who should administer the punishment of "eye for eye": the court or the individual offended? How does Jesus answer the question of retaliation for an offense (Mt 5:38-42)?

Chapter 20

For understanding
1. **20:2.** What was the job of the priest in speaking to soldiers before a battle? Why will trust in the Lord be needed when the people enter Canaan?
2. **20:5-9.** What circumstances would exempt a soldier from combat duty?
3. **20:10-18.** What would cause the rules of siege warfare to differ? What is the rule regarding subjugation? Where is extermination mandated?
4. **20:17.** What is the ban of total destruction a means of doing? Who are the Hittites and Jebusites? According to a Jewish tradition in the *Book of Jubilees*, which dates to the second century B.C., how was the world divided? Against this background, what was the reason behind Israel's conquest of Canaan?

For application
1. **20:5-8.** What circumstances or conditions would excuse a person from military duty today? What could excuse the person from engaging in battle once he is trained for it?
2. **20:13-14.** How does the Christian view of the value of human life moderate the conduct of soldiers in battle with regard to civilians? Why is it considered an atrocity among us for the victors in battle to exterminate all the males, including young boys, but to spare at least women of childbearing years?
3. **20:16-18.** Why would a God who is defined as love itself (1 Jn 4:8) impose a total ban on the current occupants of the Promised Land? What rationale does Moses give for it? How does Christian faith evaluate such a policy as part of God's plan?

Chapter 21

For understanding
1. **21:1-9.** According to the law for unsolved homicides, if the body of a murder victim is found, and the culprit remains unknown, what must the town nearest the crime scene do? What about sin is implied?
2. **21:15-17.** What does the law of primogeniture protect? Without this legal safeguard, what could a father do? While Deuteronomy does not create the right of the first-born son, what does it guard against? What various family struggles in the Book of Genesis does the law of primogeniture recall?
3. **21:22.** To what does this verse refer? Against what did this gruesome spectacle, with the body tied or impaled to a tree or wooden upright, stand as a warning? How does Deuteronomy regulate the practice?
4. **21:23.** How is the curse manifested? What do other passages imply that the criminal must bear? To what method of execution do later Jewish texts relate this punishment? Why does Paul also cite this passage in connection with the Crucifixion of Jesus?

For application
1. **21:1-9.** Why might a city where a murder was committed wish to perform an act of atonement as described here? In modern cities with high murder rates, what acts of reparation might be appropriate for parishes to perform? What acts of reparation for the deaths of unborn children are even now being performed?

2. **21:15–17.** What is your position in birth order in your family? If you are the oldest, what rights and responsibilities are or have been yours within your immediate family? If you are not the oldest, how have you regarded your place among your siblings? What does birth order have to do with any inheritance expectations you may have had?
3. **21:18.** Read the note for this verse. How have your parents disciplined you, and with what end in mind? How has their discipline of you carried over into your training of your own children? How have they grown under your discipline?

Chapter 22

For understanding
1. **22:5.** What kind of dress is forbidden? What is implied about transvestism?
2. **22:10.** Why is plowing with an ox and donkey together forbidden? In addition, how does the Torah classify each animal? When does Paul seem to allude to this law?
3. **22:22–30.** With what do these penal laws deal? Which of these sexual crimes warrant the death penalty?
4. **22:29.** In this example of a rape, why would divorce not be an option for the rapist who is forced to marry the victim?

For application
1. **22:5.** If the Lord had a complaint against today's clothing fashions, what do you think the complaint would be, and why? What would he say about the penchant for near or total public nudity?
2. **22:8.** In a litigious society like ours, for what may homeowners be liable if an accident occurs to someone on their property? According to St. Paul, how should lawsuits between Christians be settled (1 Cor 6:1–7)?
3. **22:13–17.** How important is premarital virginity to the integrity of a marriage? What has our culture lost from having lost respect for physical virginity? How does physical virginity correlate with spiritual virginity?
4. **22:25–27.** The word "rape" comes from a Latin verb meaning "to plunder" or "steal forcibly". What does a rapist steal from his victim? Even in a morally compromised age such as ours, why is rape such a heinous crime?

Chapter 23

For understanding
1. **23:1.** To what does the "assembly of the Lord" refer here? Understood in this way, to whom are liturgical festivals off-limits? When will these restrictions be lifted?
2. **23:10–14.** What are these sanitation laws designed to protect? Where must soldiers go after a nocturnal emission of semen and for defecation?
3. **23:17.** What does the law about cult prostitutes forbid? Unfortunately, what do the Books of the Kings document?
4. **23:20.** What does this law regarding interest on loans allow? What is still forbidden?

For application
1. **23:6.** Considering the context, why does Moses forbid seeking the peace and prosperity of Israel's traditional enemies? What does Jesus say about antipathy toward enemies (Mt 5:43–44)?
2. **23:15–16.** What kinds of slavery exist in our country today, despite the illegality of slavery? What human trafficking laws exist in your part of the country? How can persons freed from slavery or trafficking be cared for?
3. **23:19–20.** What is usury? Which is usurious: a loan company charging 50% interest on a short-term loan; a credit card company charging 19% interest on outstanding balances; a bank charging 3.5% interest on a mortgage? What interest would be reasonable on a loan to a fellow Christian?
4. **23:21.** What is a vow (CCC 2102)? If you make a private vow to the Lord, which no one but you knows of, what is your obligation to fulfill it?

Chapter 24

For understanding
1. **24:1–4.** What about divorce and remarriage does Deuteronomy prohibit? Without this restriction, what could a husband, who alone had the legal right to initiate divorce, be able to do? While Deuteronomy does not thereby throw open the doors to divorce, what does it rather do? Though Jesus described divorce and remarriage as a legal concession to the sinfulness of Israel, what did he do with the Mosaic permission?
2. **24:1.** What does the Hebrew translated "indecency" (literally "nakedness of a thing") concern? Why is adultery probably not intended? In later Judaism, how was the legal ground for divorce defined? What is a bill of divorce? What provisions may it have included?
3. **24:5.** What exemption does the new groom enjoy? What does this law promote?
4. **24:10.** To whom were loans normally made? What was the purpose of allowing the debtor to choose his own pledge?

For application
1. **24:4.** In the Christian dispensation, what about a second marriage after divorce might defile either spouse? How may the defilement be removed or resolved?
2. **24:14–15.** In modern times, what benefits usually factor into a wage payment? What abuses can arise in payment of a worker's wage? In Catholic social teaching, what rights does the worker have?
3. **24:16.** What is "guilt by association"? In our society, how might other family members be punished for the crime of one of the members?
4. **24:19–22.** Even though the gleaning laws described in these verses no longer apply, how may the less fortunate today benefit from whatever harvest is brought to market? For example, what organizations exist to benefit the poor based on harvest results?

Chapter 25

For understanding
1. **25:4.** What is a working ox allowed to do from the grain he is processing? What spiritual lesson does Paul draw from this passage?
2. **25:5-10.** What is the law discussed in these verses called? Though strictly optional, what does it urge a man to do for his brother's widow? What is the purpose of the new union? With what is refusal to marry the widow met? What force did the duty of the brother-in-law, here codified as law, have in patriarchal times?
3. **25:9.** What was the meaning of removing the sandal? How do some interpret the gesture?
4. **25:13-16.** What does this law address? What does justice require for all commercial transactions? What standard of measurement should be used for buying?

For application
1. **25:2.** In our court system, what factors can mitigate the severity of a sentence of punishment? How much time may elapse between sentencing and the execution of the sentence? What can delay it? How may justice be either served or abused by numerous appeals?
2. **25:5-10.** What did St. Paul recommend for the care of younger widows? Of widows over sixty (1 Tim 5:3-14)? In the Christian community, what care should be taken of widows, especially ones with no family in the immediate vicinity?
3. **25:13-16.** How well have you familiarized yourself with the techniques of con artists in our digital age? What resources are available for helping you to recognize a scam or inducement to fraud? If you have ever been scammed or hoodwinked out of money, what lesson did you learn from it?

Chapter 26

For understanding
1. **26:2.** To what does the "first of all the fruit" refer here?
2. **26:5.** Who is the "wandering Aramean"? How is his reputation as a wanderer borne out?
3. **26:12.** Which tithe is referred to here?
4. **26:14.** What problem would handling the tithe in a state of ritual impurity cause? Which food offerings for the dead are meant?

For application
1. **26:5-9.** This passage is read at most Seder celebrations to answer the youngest child's four questions about the meal. How does that practice reflect the purpose of the Liturgy of the Word at Mass? Why is it necessary to remember events of salvation history at important celebrations?
2. **26:13-14.** How do you go about sharing your material goods with the poor, for example, by donating to charitable organizations or performing a direct service? If you donate money, how do you select your charities? What motivates you?
3. **26:17-19.** In what way might you see your involvement in the Christian covenant as an exchange of persons? How does God take you to himself, and how do you take him to yourself? What does keeping the commandments have to do with this?

Chapter 27

For understanding
1. **27:1-26.** What procedures are described in this chapter? What are some ways in which the Shechem liturgy of Deut 27 mirrors the Sinai liturgy of Ex 24? However, what are some important differences? What claim in 29:1 do the differences reinforce?
2. **27:11-14.** Where will the tribes assemble, and what will they do there? Which tribes will Gerizim, the southern peak, host, and which will Ebal, the northern peak, host?
3. **27:15-26.** What does this litany of twelve curses invoked by the twelve tribes ratify? What will the priests and the people do antiphonally? Since the nature of these curses is not specified here, only the sins that trigger them, where will they be specified in detail?
4. **27:26.** To what does the final curse, which is climactic and comprehensive, apply? Why does Paul cite this final curse in Gal 3:10? When did Jesus redeem us from the curse of the Law?

For application
1. **27:1-26.** The note for this chapter explains how ratification of the Deuteronomic covenant took place. At the Easter Vigil, how do you renew your baptismal vows? Why does the Church insist on this solemn renewal?
2. **27:5-6.** According to the *Catechism*, among the Israelites the altar was the place where sacrifices were offered to God. Among Christians, what does the altar represent (CCC 1383)? Just as the Israelites offered communion sacrifices, what kind of sacrifice is offered on the Christian altar?
3. **27:15-26.** In a public setting, how is a litany, such as the Litany of the Saints, usually recited? In the litany recorded in these verses, what does the word "Amen" mean? To what does it commit the people?

Chapter 28

For understanding
1. **28:1-68.** What are the sanctions of the Deuteronomic covenant? How is it indicated that the possibilities of both blessings and curses are conditional? Where else do blessings and curses appear in ancient documents?
2. **28:49.** What nation, swift as the eagle, is meant here? Historically, which nations fulfilled this role? Which foreign tongues would these be?

3. **28:62.** Why will Israel become few in number?
4. **28:64.** When will the curse of exile become a reality?

For application
1. **28:1.** From whom do the blessings of obedience to the Lord's voice come? In the Christian life, what are the spiritual consequences of obeying the Holy Spirit (e.g., Gal 5:22–23)?
2. **28:10.** How can living a fruitful Christian life serve an evangelistic purpose? What kind of witness to unbelievers can it give?
3. **28:1–68.** Moses spends 14 verses listing the blessings of the covenant and 54 verses detailing the curses. Why this imbalance? Why the use of very graphic language in some of these curses?
4. **28:15.** What are the spiritual consequences of refusing to obey the Lord's voice (e.g., Gal 5:19–21)? How do these consequences follow from such a refusal? According to the Galatians passage, what is the source of these consequences?

Chapter 29

For understanding
1. **29:1.** To what laws do these words refer? How is the Deuteronomic covenant distinct from the Sinai covenant? Where was the Sinai covenant ratified? By contrast, where is the Deuteronomic covenant made? Where is Moab, and where did Israel make its final encampment before entering the Promised Land? For what is Horeb another name?
2. **29:3.** How old would the assembly listening to Moses have been when they witnessed the marvels of the Exodus? What would have happened to everyone over 19 years old at that time?
3. **29:4.** What is the idiom for spiritual discernment? What does Moses contend? Failing to recognize the need for grace, what would the people fail to do?
4. **29:15.** To whom is Moses referring as "him who is not here"?

For application
1. **29:4.** As Moses suggests, how does one acquire the "eyes to see or ears to hear" what the Lord is doing or saying? As you have grown in the spiritual life, how has your spiritual visual and auditory perception improved? What helps have you sought to improve your perception?
2. **29:10–13.** In addition to removing the stain of Original Sin, what does the Sacrament of Baptism do? Viewed in terms of covenant, what baptismal oaths or promises have all who receive the sacrament made?
3. **29:14–15.** Who else does the Lord wish to bring into this baptismal covenant? What is your role in bringing this wish to fulfillment?
4. **29:18–19.** What is a "Catholic in name only"? How does Paul's description in 2 Tim 3:2–5 apply to the way such people live? What danger do they pose to the rest of the Christian community?

Chapter 30

For understanding
1. **30:6.** What does this verse indicate that God will do for his people that they cannot do for themselves? What does Moses thus prophesy? How does the sentence read in the Greek LXX? What does talk of a new circumcision imply? According to St. Paul, how is this fulfilled?
2. **Word Study: Heart (30:6).** As a word meaning "heart" or "inner self", to what does the Hebrew word *lebab* or *leb* refer? Of what is the heart the seat? As the hidden center of the person, who is the only one who can see it, and how is it wounded? For this reason, why is the healing of the heart the focus of OT eschatology? Regardless of the metaphor used, what is the main point?
3. **30:11–14.** How does Moses dismiss excuses for disobedience? What does Israel lack? How does Paul apply this assessment of the Law to the word of the gospel?
4. **30:15.** What choice do the two ways of the covenant mean for Israel? According to St. Caesarius of Arles, what outcomes are contained in these two ways?

For application
1. **30:6.** When the Lord cuts away things that you hold dear, how do you respond? What is his purpose? With what does he replace them?
2. **30:11–14.** Moses says that the word of God is "in your mouth and in your heart". How is the mouth related to what is in the heart (Rom 10:9)? According to Sir 15:14–15, what in addition to faith is needed to keep the commandments?
3. **30:14.** Read the note for this verse. Likewise, how is the way of the Lord made continuously present in the life of the devout Christian?
4. **30:15, 19.** In the last analysis, why are there only two choices? Why are there ultimately no "gray areas" in the spiritual life?

Chapter 31

For understanding
1. **31:1–23.** How is leadership over Israel transferred from Moses to Joshua? When does this transfer of authority take place? Because times of transition can be times of uncertainty and fear, what words punctuate the speeches? According to Origen of Alexandria, what does the death of Moses allegorically foreshadow? Whose coming does the succession of Moses by Joshua announce?
2. **31:9.** What does this verse claim? For what other parts of the Pentateuch is Mosaic authorship claimed? How prevalent was the belief that Moses wrote the books of the Torah? Whom do witnesses to this belief in the NT include?

3. **31:11.** To what place is Moses referring, and what is to happen there? For what did ancient Near Eastern treaties also set aside time?
4. **31:26.** Where is the Deuteronomy scroll kept, and why? How is this unlike where the tablets of the Decalogue are kept?

For application
1. **31:2-6.** Whose successor is the current pope? What concerns do most people have when a pope either dies or resigns and a new one must be elected? What considerations should help answer these concerns?
2. **31:7-8.** When a new pope is elected and accepts the office, what virtues does he most need? According to custom, what do his first words try to communicate when he greets the people from the loggia?
3. **31:10-13.** Why do Christians recite the Nicene Creed during major liturgies, especially during the Easter Vigil? How does the Creed function as an act of worship, a confession, and a rule of faith?
4. **31:20.** Since it was God himself who promised the chosen people a land flowing with milk and honey and led them to it, why is he now predicting that the people will grow fat and reject him? What is the danger to the faith of a comfortable life?

Chapter 32

For understanding
1. **32:1-43.** What do the lyrics of the Song of Moses constitute? Whom does the Song vindicate, and whom does it prosecute? How does it combine elements of flashback and forecast? Although the same story of rebellion and future restoration is outlined in the prose account of 30:1-10, how does the Song frame it? When does the NT reference the Song of Moses?
2. **32:5.** How has Israel dealt corruptly with God? What bond does the Song stress? Which generation is this crooked generation like?
3. **32:8.** To what table does this verse allude? Where did these nations spread to? What did fixing the bounds of the nations suggest? What manuscripts does the RSVCE follow? How do other Greek manuscripts and the Masoretic Hebrew text read? To what different interpretations do these different wordings lend themselves?
4. **32:15.** In Deuteronomy and Isaiah, for whom is Jeshurun an epithet? How is its meaning debated? What does Moses foresee Israel doing in Canaan? According to St. John Chrysostom, once the Israelites enjoyed relief and freedom from bondage, how should they have behaved, but what instead did they do?
5. **32:21.** What does the Lord intend to provide by stirring Israel to jealousy? Who are the "no people"? How will the Lord make Israel jealous? According to Paul, when is this fulfilled? What effect will the discipline envisioned by the Song thus have?

For application
1. **32:5.** Has there ever been a generation that was not "perverse and crooked"? What is the cause of this? How can human perversity and crookedness be counteracted?
2. **32:17.** How is the paganism of our age different from that of the ancients? Which are some of the "new gods" that our generation appears to be worshiping? What are some of the spiritual roots of this new paganism?
3. **32:29.** What is mankind's "latter end"? What are the "four last things"? Why is it unwise to avoid bearing them in mind?
4. **32:36.** Read the note for this verse. When is God's mercy most likely to manifest itself in the life of a sinner? Have you ever confronted the need for mercy in your own life?

Chapter 33

For understanding
1. **33:1-29.** What blessings does Moses invoke here? How are his words like the patriarchal blessings in Genesis? What does the use of this model hint about Moses? Which tribe is omitted from the list of blessings, and why?
2. **33:8.** What are the Thummim and Urim? What did these small items, kept in the custody of the high priest, represent?
3. **33:10.** As ministers of word and sacrament in Israel, for what are the Levitical priests in the line of Aaron responsible? Why is no reference made to Levi's territory?
4. **33:22.** Where is Bashan? What did its pasturelands support and its forestlands provide cover for? What allusion do some read in this passage?

For application
1. **33:2.** The note for this verse cites Heb 2:2. What point is the author of Hebrews making about fidelity to the Christian message (Heb 2:2-4)? If the Law of Moses promised blessings for obedience and curses for disobedience, what does the future hold for those who disregard or disobey an even more powerful word?
2. **33:9.** What level of commitment does Jesus demand of his disciples (Lk 14:26)? How does Jesus' demand square with the commandment to honor father and mother? Why does a relationship with Jesus take priority over blood relations?
3. **33:12.** Why was Benjamin especially beloved of his father, Jacob (Gen 35:18; 42:4, 36-38)? How does he remind you of the Apostle John? Although the expression "beloved of the Lord" seems to imply a special status for certain individuals, how might you describe yourself as beloved of the Lord?
4. **33:26-29.** How is Christianity unique among all other religions? Even though Christians suffer persecution for their faith, how can they count themselves happy?

Chapter 34

For understanding
1. **34:1-12.** What do these verses appear to be? Which two considerations point in this direction?
2. **34:6.** Who buried Moses and where? How does the Greek LXX read, and what does it imply? What is Beth-peor?

3. **34:7.** What is the significance of a hundred and twenty years? How can the lifetime of Moses be divided? By an extraordinary grace, how did Moses appear at the time of his death?
4. **34:9.** What does the imposition of hands signal? Upon whom did Moses perform this rite?

For application
1. **34:5.** This verse gives Moses the title "servant of the Lᴏʀᴅ". What makes this a title of honor? Given the circumstances of your life, what would enable you to claim this title as your own?
2. **34:7.** In your opinion, what constitutes a full lifetime? What makes one's lifetime a success, and what makes it a failure regardless of age?
3. **34:9.** In the Christian understanding, what does the laying on of hands signify? During which of the Sacraments of Initiation were the hands of one in authority laid on you? What graces were communicated to you then, and what commission to covenant leadership did they entail?
4. **34:10.** What does the expression "face to face" signify? Why is our communication with God usually mediated through signs and symbols? According to 1 Jn 3:2, when can we expect to see God face-to-face?

BOOKS OF THE BIBLE

THE OLD TESTAMENT (OT)

Gen	Genesis
Ex	Exodus
Lev	Leviticus
Num	Numbers
Deut	Deuteronomy
Josh	Joshua
Judg	Judges
Ruth	Ruth
1 Sam	1 Samuel
2 Sam	2 Samuel
1 Kings	1 Kings
2 Kings	2 Kings
1 Chron	1 Chronicles
2 Chron	2 Chronicles
Ezra	Ezra
Neh	Nehemiah
Tob	Tobit
Jud	Judith
Esther	Esther
Job	Job
Ps	Psalms
Prov	Proverbs
Eccles	Ecclesiastes
Song	Song of Solomon
Wis	Wisdom
Sir	Sirach (Ecclesiasticus)
Is	Isaiah
Jer	Jeremiah
Lam	Lamentations
Bar	Baruch
Ezek	Ezekiel
Dan	Daniel
Hos	Hosea
Joel	Joel
Amos	Amos
Obad	Obadiah
Jon	Jonah
Mic	Micah
Nahum	Nahum
Hab	Habakkuk
Zeph	Zephaniah
Hag	Haggai
Zech	Zechariah
Mal	Malachi
1 Mac	1 Maccabees
2 Mac	2 Maccabees

THE NEW TESTAMENT (NT)

Mt	Matthew
Mk	Mark
Lk	Luke
Jn	John
Acts	Acts of the Apostles
Rom	Romans
1 Cor	1 Corinthians
2 Cor	2 Corinthians
Gal	Galatians
Eph	Ephesians
Phil	Philippians
Col	Colossians
1 Thess	1 Thessalonians
2 Thess	2 Thessalonians
1 Tim	1 Timothy
2 Tim	2 Timothy
Tit	Titus
Philem	Philemon
Heb	Hebrews
Jas	James
1 Pet	1 Peter
2 Pet	2 Peter
1 Jn	1 John
2 Jn	2 John
3 Jn	3 John
Jude	Jude
Rev	Revelation (Apocalypse)